go further with
NUMBER SKILLS

For National Curriculum levels 3-6

SPECTRUM MATHS

Dave Kirkby

Collins Educational
An imprint of HarperCollinsPublishers

© David Kirkby 1993
ISBN 000 312689 7

Published by 1993 by Collins Educational
An imprint of HarperCollins *Publishers*
77-85 Fulham Palace Road,
Hammersmith, London W6 8JB

Reprinted 1994, 1996

Illustrated by
Teri Gower

Designed by
Shireen Nathoo Design

Cover photographs of children by
Olly Hatch

Acknowledgement
We should like to thank NES Arnold Ltd, Nottingham, for kindly lending us the pictures of educational equipment for the cover.

Printed in Great Britain by
Martin's The Printers Ltd
Berwick upon Tweed

Bound in Great Britain by
Hunter & Foulis, Edinburgh

THE SPECTRUM MATHS SERIES

Starting	More	Go Further With
Investigations	Investigations	Investigations
Games	Games	Games
Data Handling	Data Handling	Data Handling
Algebra/Shape and Space	Algebra/Shape and Space	Algebra/Shape and Space
Number Skills	Number Skills	Number Skills

CONTENTS

1   The Big Wheel

2   Magic Squares

3   Grid Journeys

4   Tenths

5   Powers

6   Countdown

7   Mixed Equations

8   Nearly 20

9   5-Card Sums

10   Double See-Saw

11   Lowest Common Multiples

12   Factor Show

13   Three Stones

14   Number Puzzles

15   A Special Date

16   Multiplying Grids

17   Minus a Digit

18   Factor Grids

19   Remainder Charts

20   Multiple Percentages

21   Division Grids

22   Place Nine

23   Multiples of 10

24   Division Wheels

25   Highest Common Factors

26   Hexanimals

27   Subtraction Guessing

28   Goal Percentages

29   Consecutive Flowers

30   Fraction Wheels

31   Fractions and Decimals

32   One Hundred

33   Tridiscs

34   Multiplication Triangles

35   Mixed totals

36   Percentage Wheels

37   Five Ways

38   Take Your Pick

39   Decimal Pyramids

40   Tower Blocks

INTRODUCTION

Most schools use a mathematics scheme and teachers using these require a range of support material to supplement the scheme. Such material is provided by **Spectrum Maths**.

SPECTRUM MATHS: NUMBER SKILLS

This is a series of three books of number activities primarily for Key Stages 1 and 2, though much of it is also appropriate for Key Stage 3.

The books are defined in terms of three levels. Broadly, these levels are :
Starting Number Skills (Years 1, 2 and 3)
More Number Skills (Years 3, 4 and 5)
Go Further With Number Skills (Years 5, 6 and 7).

Each book contains:
40 pupil activities in the form of photocopymasters. There are also detailed teacher's notes accompanying each activity and Special Papers in the form of photocopymasters to help children record their work.

THE ACTIVITIES

A principal aim of mathematics teaching is to equip children to handle numbers with confidence. These activities provide an opportunity for children to practise number skills, with a strong emphasis on operational skills.

Each activity contains empty **number boxes** which children are required to complete, or sometimes colour. In most cases this is followed by an appropriate extension activity.

USING THE ACTIVITIES

The activities do not, in general, attempt to teach children the number skills they need. They provide practice and reinforcement for children who, having been introduced to the skills, need experiences to develop them.

Activities can be selected by the teacher to suit particular needs and situations. They can be used in a variety of ways:

- ► to integrate into the school mathematics programme
- ► to consolidate other work in the school mathematics scheme
- ► to provide enrichment material at appropriate times
- ► to form support material for responding to wide ranges of ability
- ► to complement other activities within the **Spectrum Maths** series.

In particular, many activities in the **Spectrum Games** and **Spectrum Investigations** series can be used in conjunction with this series to provide rich and varied opportunities for children to develop their skills.

THE TEACHER'S NOTES

The teacher's notes contain, for each activity:
- ► clear indications of the content area
- ► details of any necessary apparatus
- ► notes outlining suggestions for introducing the activities
- ► ideas for extending the activities
- ► answers to the activities
- ► clearly identifiable National Curriculum references on a grid
- ► reference to related activities within the book and other books in the **Spectrum Maths** series.

USING THE TEACHER'S NOTES

LEVEL	UA	N	SSM	HD	A
1					
2					
3					
4					
5					
6					

KEY UA Using and Applying Mathematics
       N Number
   SSM Shape, Space and Measures
    HD Handling Data
      A Algebra

This section contains answers to the activity. These appear as a reduced copy of the pupil activity sheet.

The table on the left refers to the Programmes of Study and Levels 1–6 of the National Curriculum. An algebra column has been included for teachers using this book at Key Stage 3. An attempt has been made to locate, by means of dots in the table, the approximate content level for each activity, but it must be appreciated that many activities can be performed at a variety of levels.

SKILLS

This section summarises the main content area of the activity.

APPARATUS

Details of necessary apparatus or special paper photocopymasters which are included at the back of the book

NOTE

This section contains suggestions for introducing the activity.

EXTENSION

This contains ideas for extending the activity.

SPECTRUM LINKS

	Data Handling	Games	Investigations	Algebra / S&S	Number Skills
Starting					
More		This section references related activities available throughout the Spectrum Series. The reference gives the number and title of the activity.			
Go Further With					

The Big Wheel

LEVEL	UA	N	SSM	HD	A
1					
2		●			
3		●			
4					
5					
6					

● Learning and using addition and subtraction facts.

SKILLS

► Adding three single-digit numbers
► Searching for sets of numbers which have a given total

APPARATUS

Numbered cards, 1-9

NOTE

Suggest to the children that they draw a large wheel on paper, then use numbered cards placed on the wheel to help them find solutions.

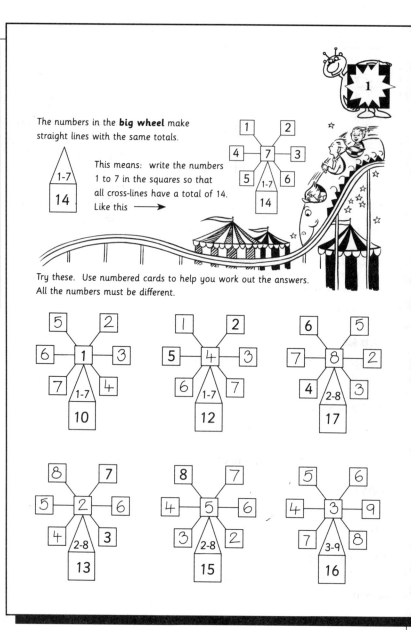

The numbers in the **big wheel** make straight lines with the same totals.

This means: write the numbers 1 to 7 in the squares so that all cross-lines have a total of 14. Like this ──▶

Try these. Use numbered cards to help you work out the answers. All the numbers must be different.

SPECTRUM LINKS

	Data Handling	Games	Investigations	Algebra/S&S	Number Skills
Starting			23 Dice Sort		
More		26 Fifteens	2 Lucky 13 11 Triplets		25 Addition Grids 34 Magic Windmills 35 Magic Triangles 38 Side Totals

The Big Wheel

The numbers in the **big wheel** make straight lines with the same totals.

This means: write the numbers 1 to 7 in the squares so that all cross-lines have a total of 14. Like this ⟶

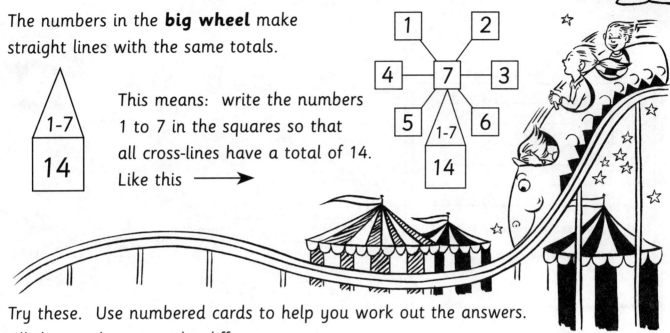

Try these. Use numbered cards to help you work out the answers. All the numbers must be different.

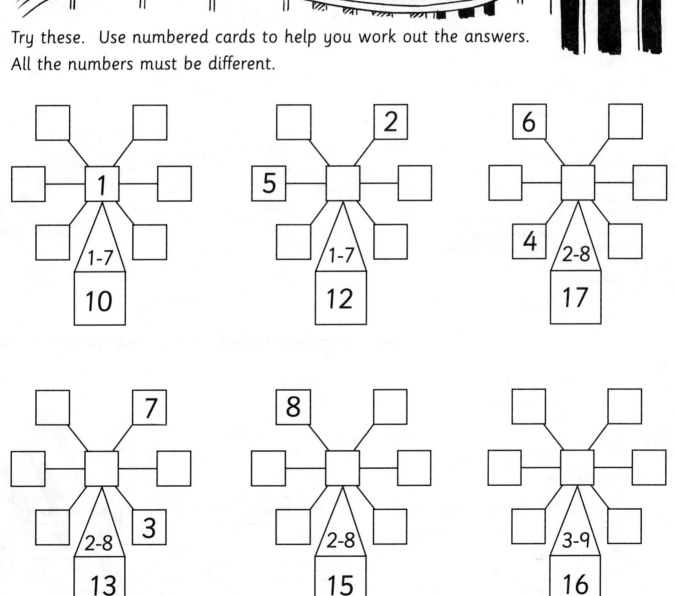

Magic Squares

LEVEL	UA	N	SSM	HD	A
1					
2		●			
3		●			
4					
5					
6					

- ● Learning and using addition and subtraction facts to 20.
- ● Adding three single-digit numbers.

SKILLS

► Adding three single-digit numbers
► Searching for arrangements of numbers within a 3 x 3 grid for given row and column totals

APPARATUS

Squared paper, scissors

NOTE

The solutions can be deduced by systematically working round the square.

EXTENSION

► Create 4 x 4 magic squares using, for example, the numbers 1-16.

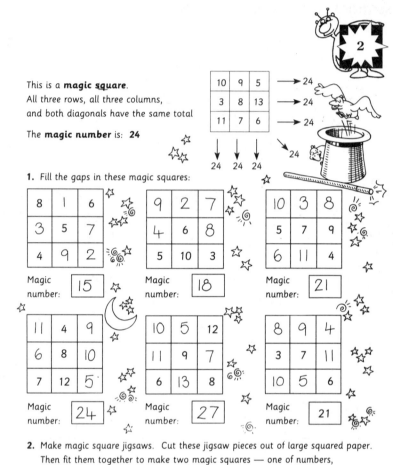

This is a **magic square**.
All three rows, all three columns, and both diagonals have the same total

The **magic number** is: 24

10	9	5	→ 24
3	8	13	→ 24
11	7	6	→ 24

↓ ↓ ↓
24 24 24

1. Fill the gaps in these magic squares:

8	1	6
3	5	7
4	9	2

Magic number: 15

9	2	7
4	6	8
5	10	3

Magic number: 18

10	3	8
5	7	9
6	11	4

Magic number: 21

11	4	9
6	8	10
7	12	5

Magic number: 24

10	5	12
11	9	7
6	13	8

Magic number: 27

8	9	4
3	7	11
10	5	6

Magic number: 21

2. Make magic square jigsaws. Cut these jigsaw pieces out of large squared paper. Then fit them together to make two magic squares — one of numbers, one of dots.

| 4 | 11 | 6 |

| 9 | 7 | 5 |

| 8 | 3 | 10 |

SPECTRUM LINKS

	Data Handling	Games	Investigations	Algebra/S&S	Number Skills
More		26 Fifteens			18 2 x 2 Addition Squares 25 Addition Grids 26 Cloud Numbers
Go Further With					22 Place Nine

Magic Squares

This is a **magic square**.
All three rows, all three columns,
and both diagonals have the same total.

The **magic number** is: **24**

10	9	5	→ 24
3	8	13	→ 24
11	7	6	→ 24

↓ 24 ↓ 24 ↓ 24   ↘ 24

1. Fill the gaps in these magic squares:

8		6
	5	
4		

Magic number: _____

	6	
5	10	3

Magic number: _____

5	7	9
		4

Magic number: _____

	4	
	8	
7	12	

Magic number: _____

		12
	9	
6		8

Magic number: _____

3	7	
		6

Magic number: 21

2. Make magic square jigsaws. Cut these jigsaw pieces out of large squared paper.
Then fit them together to make two magic squares — one of numbers,
one of dots.

| 4 | 11 | 6 |

| 9 | 7 | 5 |

| 8 | 3 | 10 |

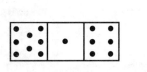

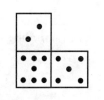

Grid Journeys

LEVEL	UA	N	SSM	HD	A
1			●		
2					
3	●				
4	●	●			
5	●				
6					

● Addition of several single-digit numbers.
● Giving and understanding instructions for movement along a route.

SKILLS

Finding a running total when adding several single-digit numbers
Following a path on a grid based on left, right, up, down movements

EXTENSION

► Ask children to draw up a larger (say, 4 x 4) grid and work out routes for friends to follow.

The **journey code** is:
U - Up (north)
D - Down (south)
L - Left (west)
R - Right (east)

A 2	B 3	C 1
D 4	E 5	F 6
G 7	H 3	I 2

If you start at E and travel URDDL, your **journey score** is
5 + 3 + 1 + 6 + 2 + 3 = 20

Find these journey scores.

1. Start at E

LUR — 14
DRU — 16
RDLL — 23
ULDRD — 22
LDRRU — 27

2. Start at B

RDDLL — 22
LRRLD — 17
LDRDR — 19
DDRUU — 20
DLDRU — 27

3. Can you find ten different journey scores starting at H?

Question 3: Some different journey scores starting at H are:

Two stages:
LU - 3 + 7 + 4 = 14
UL - 3 + 5 + 4 = 12
RU - 3 + 2 + 6 = 11
UR - 3 + 5 + 6 = 14
UU - 3 + 5 +3 = 11

Three stages:
UUR - 3 + 5 + 3 + 1 = 12
UUL - 3 + 5 + 3 + 2 = 13
URU - 3 + 5 + 6 + 1 = 15
ULU - 3 + 5 + 4 + 2 = 14
URD - 3 + 5 + 6 + 2 = 16

SPECTRUM LINKS

	Data Handling	Games	Investigations	Algebra/S&S	Number Skills
Starting					32 Number Journey

Grid Journeys

The **journey code** is:

U - Up (north)

D - Down (south)

L - Left (west)

R - Right (east)

A 2	B 3	C 1
D 4	E 5	F 6
G 7	H 3	I 2

If you start at E and travel URDDL,
your **journey score** is

5 + 3 + 1 + 6 + 2 + 3 = ⎡20⎤

Find these journey scores.

1. Start at E

LUR ⬜

DRU ⬜

RDLL ⬜

ULDRD ⬜

LDRRU ⬜

2. Start at B

RDDLL ⬜

LRRLD ⬜

LDRDR ⬜

DDRUU ⬜

DLDRU ⬜

3. Can you find ten different journey scores starting at H?

Tenths

LEVEL	UA	N	SSM	HD	A
1					
2					
3	●				
4	●	●			
5	●				
6					

● Using, with understanding, decimal notation, in the context of measurement.
● Approximating.

SKILLS

► Locating position on a number line using tenths
► Rounding decimals to the nearest whole number

APPARATUS

Squared paper

EXTENSION

► Children can be given further practice with the use of a 10-point number line on the wall. Vary the number cards at the ends of the line, for example:

Discussion will arise regarding the nearest whole number to 10.5, for example.

These number lines are marked in **tenths** or **fifths**.

1. Complete the boxes to show where the arrow points on each number line. Show it in **decimals**. The first one has been done for you.

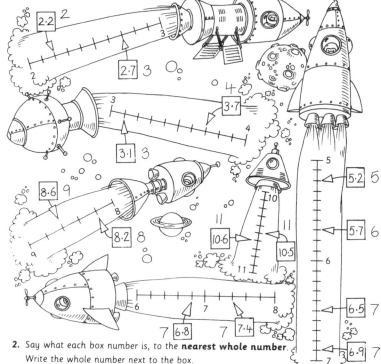

2. Say what each box number is, to the **nearest whole number**. Write the whole number next to the box.

3. Draw your own number lines using squared paper. Then draw boxes to show the position of some numbers. Ask a friend to fill in the boxes.

SPECTRUM LINKS

	Data Handling	Games	Investigations	Algebra/S&S	Number Skills
More					**11** Temperature Scales **27** Nearest 100 **29** Nearest 10
Go Further With	**9** Inches and Centimetres **18** Miles and Kilometres	**12** Decimate **14** Two Places **37** Four Rounds	**20** Nearest Wholes		**31** Fractions and Decimals **39** Decimal Pyramids

Tenths

These number lines are marked in **tenths** or **fifths**.

1. Complete the boxes to show where the arrow points on each number line.
Show it in **decimals**. The first one has been done for you.

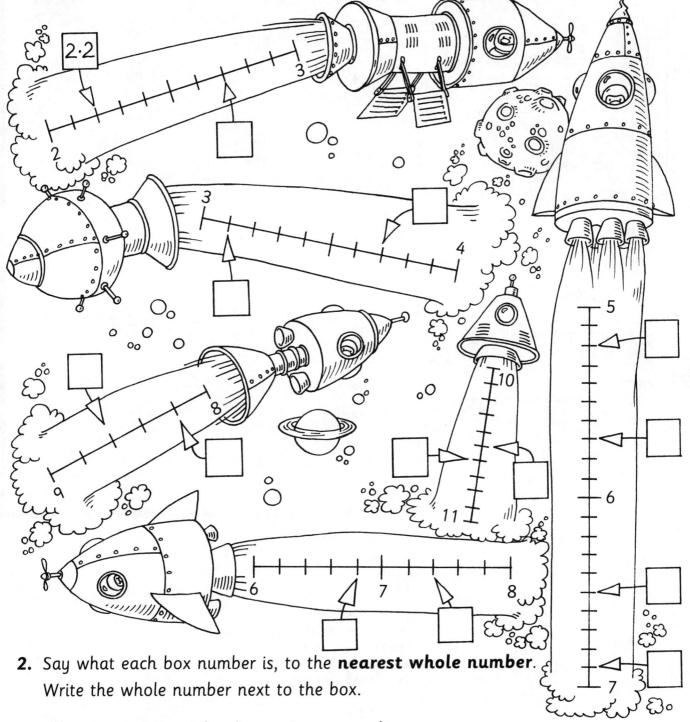

2. Say what each box number is, to the **nearest whole number**.
Write the whole number next to the box.

3. Draw your own number lines using squared paper.
Then draw boxes to show the position of some numbers.
Ask a friend to fill in the boxes.

SPECTRUM MATHS ■ GO FURTHER WITH NUMBER SKILLS

5

Powers

LEVEL	UA	N	SSM	HD	A
1					
2					
3	●	●			
4	●	●			
5	●				
6					

- ● Learning multiplication facts up to 10×10 and using them in multiplication and division problems.
- ● Explaining number patterns and predicting subsequent numbers.
- ● Generalising, mainly in words, patterns which arise, eg 'square'.

SKILLS

► Expressing numbers using power notation

APPARATUS

Calculators

NOTES

Children may need help with the idea of 'to the power of one'. They may also need the term 'units digit' explained.

3^4 is a short way of writing 3 x 3 x 3 x 3 = 81. This is called 'three **to the power of** four'.

2^6 is a short way of writing 2 x 2 x 2 x 2 x 2 x 2 = 64 This is called 'two **to the power of** six'.

1. Complete these boxes. One has been done for you.

Powers of 2	Powers of 3	Powers of 4
$2^1 =$ 2	$3^1 =$ 3	$4^1 =$ 4
$2^2 =$ 4	$3^2 =$ 9	$4^2 =$ 16
$2^3 =$ 8	$3^3 =$ 27	$4^3 =$ 64
$2^4 =$ 16	$3^4 =$ 81	$4^4 =$ 256
$2^5 =$ 32	$3^5 =$ 243	$4^5 =$ 1024

2. Write down some powers of 5 and 10.
Write down some powers of other numbers. Now complete these boxes:

$2^{\boxed{3}} = 8$ $2^{\boxed{7}} = 128$ $6^{\boxed{2}} = 36$

$3^{\boxed{5}} = 243$ $4^{\boxed{4}} = 256$ $5^{\boxed{3}} = 125$

$7^{\boxed{2}} = 49$ $10^{\boxed{5}} = 1000,000$ $11^{\boxed{3}} = 1331$

3. The powers of 3 are: 3, 9, 27, 81, 243 ...and then what?
The **units digits** of these are: 3, 9, 7, 1, 3 ...and then what?

4. Do they form a pattern?
Investigate the units digits of powers of other numbers.

Question 3: 729; 9
Question 4: The patterns in the units digits of powers are:
Powers of 2: 2, 4, 8, 6, ...
Powers of 3: 3, 9, 7, 1, ...
Powers of 4: 4, 6, 4, 6, ...
Powers of 5: 5, 5, 5, 5, ...
Powers of 6: 6, 6, 6, 6, ...
Powers of 7: 7, 9, 3, 1, ...
Powers of 8: 8, 4, 2, 6, ...
Powers of 9: 9, 1, 9, 1, ...

Powers

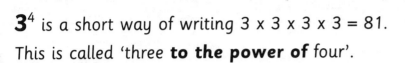

5

3^4 is a short way of writing 3 x 3 x 3 x 3 = 81.
This is called 'three **to the power of** four'.

2^6 is a short way of writing 2 x 2 x 2 x 2 x 2 x 2 = 64
This is called 'two **to the power of** six'.

1. Complete these boxes. One has been done for you.

Powers of 2	Powers of 3	Powers of 4
$2^1 = \boxed{}$	$3^1 = \boxed{}$	$4^1 = \boxed{}$
$2^2 = \boxed{}$	$3^2 = \boxed{}$	$4^2 = \boxed{}$
$2^3 = \boxed{}$	$3^3 = \boxed{}$	$4^3 = \boxed{}$
$2^4 = \boxed{}$	$3^4 = \boxed{81}$	$4^4 = \boxed{}$
$2^5 = \boxed{}$	$3^5 = \boxed{}$	$4^5 = \boxed{}$

2. Write down some powers of 5 and 10.
   Write down some powers of other numbers. Now complete these boxes:

$2^{\boxed{}} = 8$ $2^{\boxed{}} = 128$ $6^{\boxed{}} = 36$

$3^{\boxed{}} = 243$ $4^{\boxed{}} = 256$ $5^{\boxed{}} = 125$

$7^{\boxed{}} = 49$ $10^{\boxed{}} = 1000,000$ $11^{\boxed{}} = 1331$

3. The powers of 3 are: 3, 9, 27, 81, 243 ...and then what?
   The **units digits** of these are: 3, 9, 7, 1, 3 ...and then what?

4. Do they form a pattern?
   Investigate the units digits of powers of other numbers.

Countdown

LEVEL	UA	N	SSM	HD	A
1					
2					
3	●	●			
4	●	●			
5	●				
6					

● Addition, subtraction, and multiplication.
● Approximating.

SKILLS

▶ Writing expressions for numbers using combinations of a given set of digits and operations

NOTE

If children cannot find a solution, then they must aim to be as close as possible.

EXTENSION

▶ Ask the children to work with the first set of useful numbers, and suggest they try to make as many target numbers as possible, within a particular range (100-200, for example).

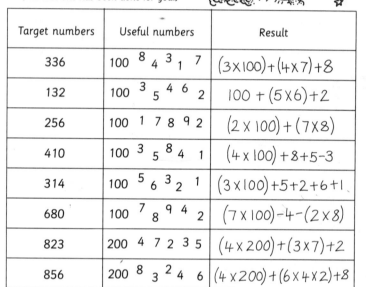

These **target numbers** can be made from the **useful numbers**.

1. Try these. Use each **useful number** once only in a line.
   You can use multiplication, addition and subtraction.
   How many of these ten targets can you reach?
   Write your answers in the **results** column.
   (The first one has been done for you.)

Target numbers	Useful numbers	Result
336	100 ^{8} 4 ^{3} 1 7	$(3 \times 100) + (4 \times 7) + 8$
132	100 ^{3} 5 ^{4} ^{6} 2	$100 + (5 \times 6) + 2$
256	100 ^{1} 7 8 ^{9} 2	$(2 \times 100) + (7 \times 8)$
410	100 ^{3} 5 ^{8} 4 1	$(4 \times 100) + 8 + 5 - 3$
314	100 ^{5} 6 ^{3} 2 1	$(3 \times 100) + 5 + 2 + 6 + 1$
680	100 ^{7} $_8$ ^{9} 4 2	$(7 \times 100) - 4 - (2 \times 8)$
823	200 4 7 2 3 5	$(4 \times 200) + (3 \times 7) + 2$
856	200 ^{8} 3 ^{2} 4 6	$(4 \times 200) + (6 \times 4 \times 2) + 8$
525	100 ^{2} 7 1 4 5	$(5 \times 100) + (4 \times 7) - 2 - 1$
186	100 2 ^{6} 7 5 4	$(2 \times 100) - 5 - 6 - 7 + 4$

2. Invent a set of your own target numbers and useful numbers.
   See how many targets you can reach.

SPECTRUM LINKS

	Data Handling	Games	Investigations	Algebra/S&S	Number Skills
Starting		13 Big Match 18 Summary 27 Choosy	10 Trios 12 Keep Your Balance 14 Card Tricks	6 Shape Search 10 Stroking Cats 15 Hunt the Numbers	
More		3 Boxer 8 Dice Superstars	29 Asking Questions	10 Mystery People	15 Dice Lines 20 Equation Solving 28 Arch Numbers 31 Target Practice
Go Further With		8 A Mouthful 33 Challenge 38 Switch	16 Number Nine 21 Equations 33 Signs	7 Number Tricks 10 Think of a Number 14 Whodunnit?	7 Mixed Equations 13 Three Stones 15 A Special Date

Countdown

These **target numbers** can be made from the **useful numbers**.

1. Try these. Use each **useful number** once only in a line.
   You can use multiplication, addition and subtraction.
   How many of these ten targets can you reach?
   Write your answers in the **results** column.
   (The first one has been done for you.)

Target numbers	Useful numbers	Result
336	100 8 4 3 1 7	(3×100)+(4×7)+8
132	100 3 5 4 6 2	
256	100 1 7 8 9 2	
410	100 3 5 8 4 1	
314	100 5 6 3 2 1	
680	100 7 8 9 4 2	
823	200 4 7 2 3 5	
856	200 8 3 2 4 6	
525	100 2 7 1 4 5	
186	100 2 6 7 5 4	

2. Invent a set of your own target numbers and useful numbers.
   See how many targets you can reach.

Mixed Equations

LEVEL	UA	N	SSM	HD	A
1					
2					
3	●	●			
4	●	●			
5	●	●			
6					

- ● Addition, subtraction, multiplication and division.
- ● Simple equations.

SKILLS

► Finding solutions to a variety of different equations with three missing digits to be selected from four

► Adding, subtracting, multiplying, dividing, and combinations of these

NOTE

Discuss the need for brackets and encourage children to use these when they are creating their own equations.

These are called **mixed equations** because they use a mixture of signs. In each equation, fill in the boxes by choosing three numbers from the four in the picture. They must all be different from each other.

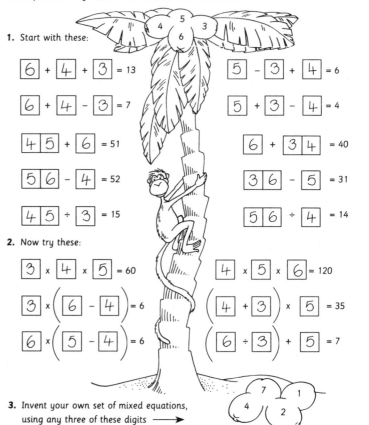

1. Start with these:

$\boxed{6} + \boxed{4} + \boxed{3} = 13$ $\boxed{5} - \boxed{3} + \boxed{4} = 6$

$\boxed{6} + \boxed{4} - \boxed{3} = 7$ $\boxed{5} + \boxed{3} - \boxed{4} = 4$

$\boxed{4}\boxed{5} + \boxed{6} = 51$ $\boxed{6} + \boxed{3}\boxed{4} = 40$

$\boxed{5}\boxed{6} - \boxed{4} = 52$ $\boxed{3}\boxed{6} - \boxed{5} = 31$

$\boxed{4}\boxed{5} \div \boxed{3} = 15$ $\boxed{5}\boxed{6} \div \boxed{4} = 14$

2. Now try these:

$\boxed{3} \times \boxed{4} \times \boxed{5} = 60$ $\boxed{4} \times \boxed{5} \times \boxed{6} = 120$

$\boxed{3} \times (\boxed{6} - \boxed{4}) = 6$ $(\boxed{4} + \boxed{3}) \times \boxed{5} = 35$

$\boxed{6} \times (\boxed{5} - \boxed{4}) = 6$ $(\boxed{6} \div \boxed{3}) + \boxed{5} = 7$

3. Invent your own set of mixed equations, using any three of these digits ⟶

SPECTRUM LINKS

	Data Handling	Games	Investigations	Algebra/S&S	Number Skills
Starting		13 Big Match 18 Summary 27 Choosy	10 Trios 12 Keep Your Balance 14 Card Tricks	6 Shape Search 10 Stroking Cats 15 Hunt the Numbers	
More		3 Boxer 8 Dice Superstars	29 Asking Questions	10 Mystery People	15 Dice Lines 20 Equation Solving 28 Arch Numbers 31 Target Practice
Go Further With		8 A Mouthful 33 Challenge 38 Switch	16 Number Nine 21 Equations 33 Signs	7 Number Tricks 10 Think of a Number 14 Whodunnit?	6 Countdown 13 Three Stones 15 A Special Date

Mixed Equations

These are called **mixed equations** because they use a mixture of signs. In each equation, fill in the boxes by choosing three numbers from the four in the picture. They must all be different from each other.

1. Start with these:

$\boxed{6} + \boxed{4} + \boxed{3} = 13$

$\boxed{} + \boxed{} - \boxed{} = 7$

$\boxed{} + \boxed{} = 51$

$\boxed{} - \boxed{} = 52$

$\boxed{} \div \boxed{} = 15$

$\boxed{} - \boxed{} + \boxed{} = 6$

$\boxed{} + \boxed{} - \boxed{} = 4$

$\boxed{} + \boxed{} = 40$

$\boxed{} - \boxed{} = 31$

$\boxed{} \div \boxed{} = 14$

2. Now try these:

$\boxed{} \times \boxed{} \times \boxed{} = 60$

$\boxed{} \times \left(\boxed{} - \boxed{} \right) = 6$

$\boxed{} \times \left(\boxed{} - \boxed{} \right) = 6$

$\boxed{} \times \boxed{} \times \boxed{} = 120$

$\left(\boxed{} + \boxed{} \right) \times \boxed{} = 35$

$\left(\boxed{} \div \boxed{} \right) + \boxed{} = 7$

3. Invent your own set of mixed equations, using any three of these digits ⟶

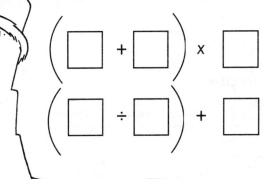

8

Nearly 20

8

LEVEL	UA	N	SSM	HD	A
1					
2					
3	●				
4	●	●			
5	●				
6					

● Adding and subtracting two two-digit numbers.
● Estimating and approximating to check the validity of addition and subtraction calculations.

SKILLS

► Subtracting two-digit numbers
► Creating subtractions by selecting from a choice of digits to give a particular answer

APPARATUS

Numbered cards, 1-9

NOTE

This activity can be started by drawing a large outline of the subtraction on a piece of paper, selecting the appropriate numbered cards, and then trying different arrangements to produce the best solution.

EXTENSION

► Ask children to explore how many different answers can be created for any one set of numbers.

1. Choose four digits from the cloud. Make them into two numbers, and subtract one from the other. Aim to get as close to 20 as possible. Record the result, and then the **difference** between it and 20. Like this ➤

2. Choose from these five digits, and see how near you can get to these numbers: 5, 10, 15, 20, 25, 30, 35, 40, 45, 50, 55, 60, 65, 70, 75, 80

SPECTRUM LINKS

	Data Handling	Games	Investigations	Algebra/S&S	Number Skills
Starting			17 Totals		
More			25 4-Card Fun		7 What's Missing? 22 Nearly 60 36 Differences
Go Further With					9 5-Card Sums 17 Minus a Digit 27 Subtraction Guessing 35 Mixed Totals

Nearly 20

8

1. Choose four digits from the cloud.
Make them into two numbers,
and subtract one from the other.
Aim to get as close to 20 as possible.
Record the result, and then the
difference between it and 20. Like this ➞

```
  5 | 7
-
  3 | 6
-----
  2   1
```

Difference: | 1 |

Difference:

Difference:

Difference:

Difference:

2. Choose from these five digits, and see how near you can get to these numbers: 5, 10, 15, 20, 25, 30, 35, 40, 45, 50, 55, 60, 65, 70, 75, 80

5-Card Sums

LEVEL	UA	N	SSM	HD	A
1					
2					
3	●				
4	●	●			
5	●				
6					

● Adding two two-digit numbers.
● Estimating and approximating to check the validity of addition and subtraction calculations.

SKILLS

► Adding a single-digit number to a two-digit number
► Arranging five digits to create both the addition and the result

APPARATUS

Numbered cards, 1-9

NOTES

Start by asking children to draw a large outline of the addition on a piece of paper. Then select the appropriate numbered cards for each addition and arrange them in search of a solution.

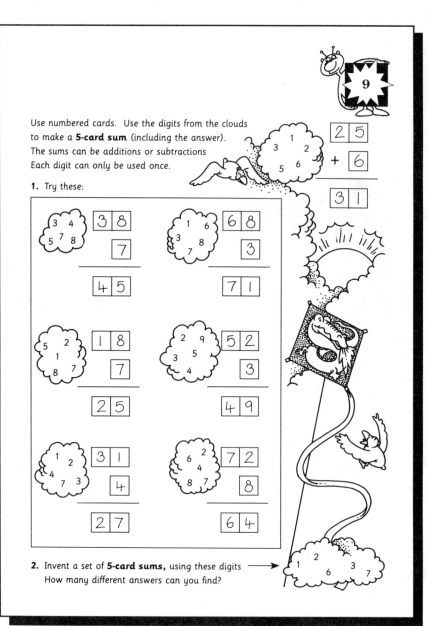

Use numbered cards. Use the digits from the clouds to make a **5-card sum** (including the answer). The sums can be additions or subtractions Each digit can only be used once.

1. Try these:

2. Invent a set of **5-card sums,** using these digits → How many different answers can you find?

SPECTRUM LINKS

	Data Handling	Games	Investigations	Algebra/S&S	Number Skills
Starting			17 Totals		
More			25 4-Card Fun		7 What's Missing? 22 Nearly 60 36 Differences
Go Further With					8 Nearly 20 17 Minus a Digit 27 Subtraction Guessing 35 Mixed Totals

5-Card Sums

Use numbered cards. Use the digits from the clouds
to make a **5-card sum** (including the answer).
The sums can be additions or subtractions
Each digit can only be used once.

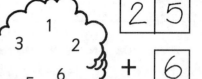

1. Try these:

2. Invent a set of **5-card sums,** using these digits ➔
How many different answers can you find?

Double See-Saws

LEVEL	UA	N	SSM	HD	A
1					
2		●			
3	●	●			
4	●				
5	●				
6					

● Learning and using addition and subtraction facts.

SKILLS

► Matching one number to the total of several others

APPARATUS

Numbered cards, 1-20

NOTES

Suggest to children that they draw a picture of a large double see-saw and use numbered cards on this to help them find answers. Note that the left-hand number must be even, for whole number solutions.

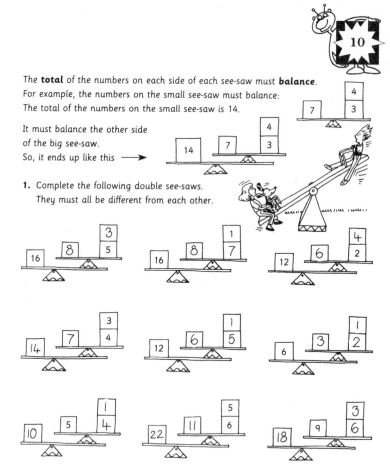

The **total** of the numbers on each side of each see-saw must **balance**. For example, the numbers on the small see-saw must balance: The total of the numbers on the small see-saw is 14.

It must balance the other side of the big see-saw. So, it ends up like this ➞

1. Complete the following double see-saws. They must all be different from each other.

2. Can you find four different solutions to the last see-saw in question one?

3. Can you find four different ways of balancing numbers, none of which are more than 10?

4. Can you find some ways of balancing numbers which are all even?

Question 2: possible solutions include 1 and 8, 2 and 7, 3 and 6, 4 and 5 on the right-hand arm of the small see-saw.
Question 3: balance 10 with 5 and 2 + 3 and with 5 and 1 + 4. Balance 8 with 4 and 3 + 1. Balance 6 with 3 and 1 + 2.
Question 4: possible solutions include: balancing 20 with 10 and 4 + 6; and balancing 16 with 8 and 6 + 2.

SPECTRUM LINKS

	Data Handling	Games	Investigations	Algebra/S&S	Number Skills
Starting			12 Keep Your Balance		30 3-Number See-Saws 37 4-Number See-Saws
More					2 Pairs See-Saw

Double See-Saws

The **total** of the numbers on each side of each see-saw must **balance**.
For example, the numbers on the small see-saw must balance:
The total of the numbers on the small see-saw is 14.

It must balance the other side
of the big see-saw.
So, it ends up like this ⟶

| 4 |
| 7 | 3 |

| 14 | 7 | 4 |
| | | 3 |

1. Complete the following double see-saws.
They must all be different from each other.

| 16 | | 5 |
| | | |

| 16 | | 1 |
| | | |

| 12 | | 2 |
| | | |

| | | 3 |
| | | 4 |

| 12 | | |
| | | |

| 6 | | |
| | | |

| | 5 | |
| | | |

| | | 5 |
| | | 6 |

| | 9 | |
| | | |

2. Can you find four different solutions to the last see-saw in question one?

3. Can you find four different ways of balancing numbers,
none of which are more than 10?

4. Can you find some ways of balancing numbers which are all even?

Lowest Common Multiples

LEVEL	UA	N	SSM	HD	A
1					
2					
3	●				
4	●	●			
5	●				
6					

● Multiplication facts up to 10 × 10.
● Patterns in multiples.

SKILLS

► Finding the lowest common multiple of two numbers

NOTES

Ask the children to discuss any pattern they find in the table. Which numbers most often appear in the table as lowest common multiples?

EXTENSION

► The activity could be extended to multiples of numbers greater than 10.

To find the **lowest common multiples** of 3 and 4: look in the x 3 row, **and** in the x 4 row.
List all the numbers you see in both (12, 24, 36, etc.) and then choose the lowest one. It is **12**.

Now list the numbers which appear in both the x 6 row and the x 10 row. Find the lowest common multiple of 6 and 10. It is 30.
These lowest common multiples are written in the table below.

x2	2	4	6	8	10	12	14	16	18	20
x3	3	6	9	12	15	18	21	24	27	30
x4	4	8	12	16	20	24	28	32	36	40
x5	5	10	15	20	25	30	35	40	45	50
x6	6	12	18	24	30	36	42	48	54	60
x7	7	14	21	28	35	42	49	56	63	70
x8	8	16	24	32	40	48	56	64	72	80
x9	9	18	27	36	45	54	63	72	81	90
x10	10	20	30	40	50	60	70	80	90	100

1. Now find some lowest common multiples for yourself.
   First, choose one of the numbers on the left of the table below.
   Then choose a number from along the bottom.
   Using the table above, find the lowest common multiple of these two numbers.
   When you have found it, write it on the table, in the right square.

2. Find the rest of the lowest common multiples to complete the table.

10	10	30	20	10	30	70	40	90	10
9	18	9	36	45	18	63	72	9	90
8	8	24	16	40	24	56	8	72	40
7	14	21	28	35	42	7	56	63	70
6	6	6	12	30	6	42	24	18	30
5	10	15	20	5	30	35	40	45	10
4	4	12	4	20	12	28	16	36	20
3	6	3	12	15	6	21	24	9	30
2	2	6	4	10	6	14	8	18	10
	2	3	4	5	6	7	8	9	10

SPECTRUM LINKS

	Data Handling	Games	Investigations	Algebra/S&S	Number Skills
More			6 Table Patterns 8 Table Ends	6 Multiple Gaps 12 Sift the Multiples 18 Patterns With 9	16 Factor Pairs 26 Cloud Numbers 33 The Right Boxes
Go Further With	26 Sevens 36 Multiplication Tables	17 Fives and Threes 24 Multiple Choice	13 Tables 37 Multiples	17 Factor Graph	20 Multiple Percentages

Lowest Common Multiples

To find the **lowest common multiples** of 3 and 4: look in the x 3 row, **and** in the x 4 row.

List all the numbers you see in both (12, 24, 36, etc.) and then choose the lowest one. It is **12**.

Now list the numbers which appear in both the x 6 row and the x 10 row. Find the lowest common multiple of 6 and 10. It is 30.

These lowest common multiples are written in the table below.

x2	2	4	6	8	10	12	14	16	18	20
x3	3	6	9	12	15	18	21	24	27	30
x4	4	8	12	16	20	24	28	32	36	40
x5	5	10	15	20	25	30	35	40	45	50
x6	6	12	18	24	30	36	42	48	54	60
x7	7	14	21	28	35	42	49	56	63	70
x8	8	16	24	32	40	48	56	64	72	80
x9	9	18	27	36	45	54	63	72	81	90
x10	10	20	30	40	50	60	70	80	90	100

1. Now find some lowest common multiples for yourself.
First, choose one of the numbers on the left of the table below.
Then choose a number from along the bottom.
Using the table above, find the lowest common multiple of these two numbers.
When you have found it, write it on the table, in the right square.

2. Find the rest of the lowest common multiples to complete the table.

	2	3	4	5	6	7	8	9	10
10									
9									
8									
7									
6									30
5			20						
4		12							
3									
2									

12

Factor Show

LEVEL	UA	N	SSM	HD	A
1					
2					
3	●				
4	●	●			
5	●				
6					

● Multiplication and division facts.
● Factors.

SKILLS

► Searching for and recording factors of different numbers

APPARATUS

Squared paper (for the extension)

NOTES

Using a multiplication square can help in the search for factors, particularly with numbers beyond 24. The resulting charts can provide a useful display to help with the exploration of factors and primes.

EXTENSIONS

► Point out to children that most numbers have two or four factors. Ask, *Which do not?*
► Ask children to make an extended table on squared paper, to show factors of numbers greater than 24.

This is a chart to show the **factors** of the numbers 1 to 24.
The factors of 8 and 21 have been filled in for you. Can you work out how?

This shows that the factors of 8 are: 1, 2, 4 and 8

This shows that 1, 3, 7 and 21 are the factors of 21.

1. Complete the table by writing in the factors of all the numbers from 1 to 24.

2. Write about anything you notice.
   Which numbers have the most factors? Which the least?

SPECTRUM LINKS

	Data Handling	Games	Investigations	Algebra/S&S	Number Skills
More		37 Snake Bite 38 Divido	6 Table Patterns 7 Pick Your Cards 8 Table Ends	8 Completing Rectangles 12 Sift the Multiples 13 Table Patterns	16 Factor Pairs 26 Cloud Numbers
Go Further With		13 Race Track 20 Factor 24 Multiple Choice	9 Factors 13 Tables	4 Prime Numbers 17 Factor Graph 18 Multiplication Machines	11 Lowest Common Multiples 18 Factor Grids 25 Highest Common Factors

Factor Show

This is a chart to show the **factors** of the numbers 1 to 24.

The factors of 8 and 21 have been filled in for you. Can you work out how?

This shows that the factors
of 8 are: 1, 2, 4 and 8

This shows that 1, 3, 7 and
21 are the factors of 21.

1. Complete the table by writing in the factors of all the numbers from 1 to 24.

2. Write about anything you notice.
    Which numbers have the most factors? Which the least?

Three Stones

LEVEL	UA	N	SSM	HD	A
1					
2					
3	●	●			
4	●	●			
5	●	●			●
6					

● Addition, subtraction, multiplication and division.
● Simple equations.

SKILLS

► Creating expressions for numbers using combined operations of addition, subtraction, multiplication and division

EXTENSION

► Ask the children to explore as many different solutions as can be found from a given number. For example:

18

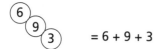 = 6 + 12

(7)(9)(2) = 7 + 9 + 2

(6)
(9)
(3) = 6 + 9 + 3

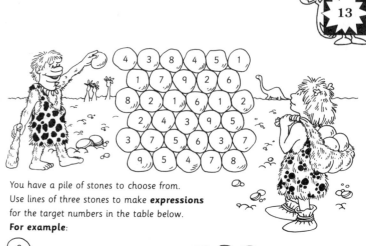

You have a pile of stones to choose from.
Use lines of three stones to make **expressions** for the target numbers in the table below.
For example:

(2)
(4)
(5)   Target number: 13   Expression: (2 × 4) +5

(6)(1)(2)   Target number: 18   Expression: 6 + 12

1. Write in as many expressions for the target numbers in the table as you can.

Target number	Expression	Target number	Expression
13	(2 × 4) +5	18	6 + 12
8	4 + 5 − 1	24	(9 × 2) + 6
14	2 + 7 + 5	19	13 + 6
6	(4 + 2) × 1	23	(8 × 2) + 7
25	(6 × 3) + 7	44	45 − 1
10	9 + 5 − 4	28	(3 × 8) + 4
72	(7 + 5) × 6	51	(6 × 9) − 3

2. Make a new table. Write in some different target numbers and try again.

SPECTRUM LINKS

	Data Handling	Games	Investigations	Algebra/S&S	Number Skills
Starting		13 Big Match 18 Summary 27 Choosy	10 Trios 12 Keep Your Balance 14 Card Tricks	6 Shape Search 10 Stroking Cats 15 Hunt the Numbers	
More		3 Boxer 8 Dice Superstars	29 Asking Questions	10 Mystery People	15 Dice Lines 20 Equation Solving 28 Arch Numbers 31 Target Practice
Go Further With		8 A Mouthful 33 Challenge 38 Switch	16 Number Nine 21 Equations 33 Signs	7 Number Tricks 10 Think of a Number 14 Whodunnit?	6 Countdown 7 Mixed Equations 15 A Special Date

Three Stones

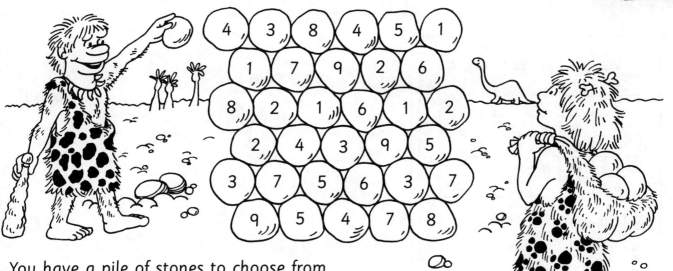

You have a pile of stones to choose from.
Use lines of three stones to make **expressions**
for the target numbers in the table below.

For example:

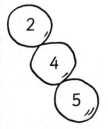

Target
number

Expression

13

$(2 \times 4) + 5$

6 1 2

Target
number

Expression

$6 + 12$

18

1. Write in as many expressions for the target numbers in the table as you can.

Target number	Expression	Target number	Expression
13	(2 X 4) +5	18	6 + 12
8		24	
14		19	
6		23	
25		44	
10		28	
72		51	

2. Make a new table. Write in some different target numbers and try again.

SPECTRUM MATHS ■ GO FURTHER WITH NUMBER SKILLS

Number Puzzles

LEVEL	UA	N	SSM	HD	A
1					
2					
3	●	●			
4	●	●			
5	●	●			
6					

- Learning and using addition and subtraction facts.
- Using 'trial and improvement' methods.

SKILLS

► Adding and subtracting

NOTES

The first three are straightforward. The next three can be solved by working round the puzzle from one corner. The second group can be approached by trial and error. In some of these cases, more than one solution is possible. For example, the first one in this group:

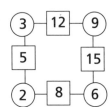

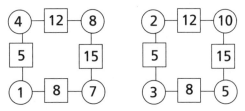

SPECTRUM LINKS

	Data Handling	Games	Investigations	Algebra/S&S	Number Skills
More					**24** Triangle Sums
Go Further With					**34** Multiplication Triangles

If you add two numbers in **circles**, you get the number between them, in a **square**.

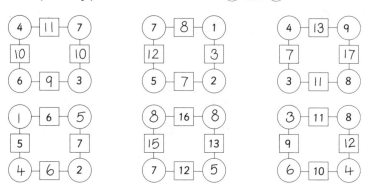

1. Complete the gaps in these.

2. And these.

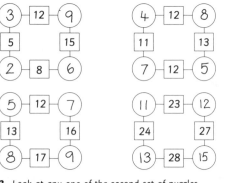

3. Look at any one of the second set of puzzles. Can you find a different solution to the same puzzle?

Number Puzzles

If you add two numbers in **circles**,
you get the number between them, in a **square**.

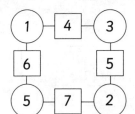

1. Complete the gaps in these.

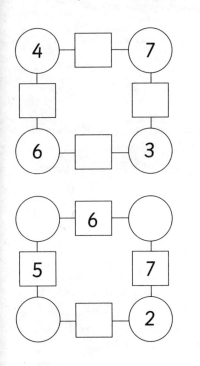

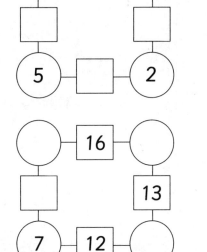

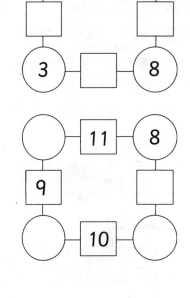

2. And these.

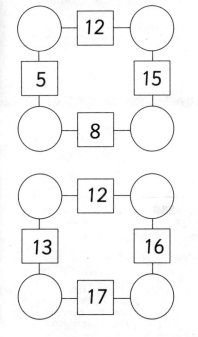

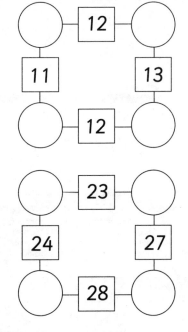

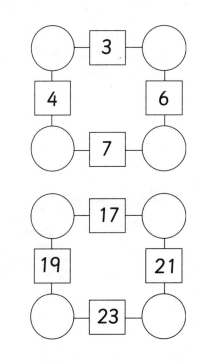

3. Look at any one of the second set of puzzles.
Can you find a different solution to the same puzzle?

A Special Date

LEVEL	UA	N	SSM	HD	A
1					
2					
3	●				
4	●	●			
5	●	●			●
6					

● Addition, subtraction, multiplication and division.
● Simple equations.

SKILLS

► Creating expressions for different numbers using a set of digits and a choice of operation signs

APPARATUS

Special Paper 1 for the extension

EXTENSION

► Continue the activity using Special Paper 1.

1. Choose a date when something special happened, (not your birthdate). Suppose you choose: **23. 3. 93**

   Keeping the date digits in order and using signs, see how many different numbers you can make.
   For example: $2 + 3 + 3 + 9 + 3 = 20$
   $2 + 3 + 3 + 9 - 3 = 14$
   $23 - 3 - 9 - 3 = 8$
   $23 + 3 - 9 + 3 = 20$

2. Colour each number on this hundred square that you can make from your date. Write down how you made it. See how many of the numbers you can colour.

1	2	3	4	5	6	7	8	9	10
11	12	13	14	15	16	17	18	19	20
21	22	23	24	25	26	27	28	29	30
31	32	33	34	35	36	37	38	39	40
41	42	43	44	45	46	47	48	49	50
51	52	53	54	55	56	57	58	59	60
61	62	63	64	65	66	67	68	69	70
71	72	73	74	75	76	77	78	79	80
81	82	83	84	85	86	87	88	89	90
91	92	93	94	95	96	97	98	99	100

3. Try again using your birthdate.

SPECTRUM LINKS

	Data Handling	Games	Investigations	Algebra/S&S	Number Skills
Starting		**13** Big Match **18** Summary **27** Choosy	**10** Trios **12** Keep Your Balance **14** Card Tricks	**6** Shape Search **10** Stroking Cats **15** Hunt the Numbers	
More		**3** Boxer **8** Dice Superstars	**29** Asking Questions	**10** Mystery People	**15** Dice Lines **20** Equation Solving **28** Arch Numbers **31** Target Practice
Go Further With		**8** A Mouthful **33** Challenge **38** Switch	**16** Number Nine **21** Equations **33** Signs	**7** Number Tricks **10** Think of a Number **14** Whodunnit?	**6** Countdown **7** Mixed Equations **13** Three Stones

A Special Date

1. Choose a date when something special happened, (not your birthdate).
Suppose you choose: **23. 3. 93**

Keeping the date digits in order and using signs, see how many different numbers you can make.

For example:　$2 + 3 + 3 + 9 + 3 = 20$
　　　　　　　$2 + 3 + 3 + 9 - 3 = 14$
　　　　　　　$23 - 3 - 9 - 3 = 8$
　　　　　　　$23 + 3 - 9 + 3 = 20$

2. Colour each number on this hundred square that you can make from your date. Write down how you made it. See how many of the numbers you can colour.

1	2	3	4	5	6	7	8	9	10
11	12	13	14	15	16	17	18	19	20
21	22	23	24	25	26	27	28	29	30
31	32	33	34	35	36	37	38	39	40
41	42	43	44	45	46	47	48	49	50
51	52	53	54	55	56	57	58	59	60
61	62	63	64	65	66	67	68	69	70
71	72	73	74	75	76	77	78	79	80
81	82	83	84	85	86	87	88	89	90
91	92	93	94	95	96	97	98	99	100

3. Try again using your birthdate.

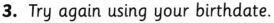

AUGUST

S	M	T	W	T	F	S
1	2	3	4	5	6	7
⑧	9	10	11	12	13	14
15	16	17	18	19	20	21
22	23	24	25	26	27	28
29	30	31				

SPECTRUM MATHS ■ GO FURTHER WITH NUMBER SKILLS

Multiplying Grids

LEVEL	UA	N	SSM	HD	A
1					
2					
3	●				
4	●	●			
5	●				
6					

● Learning multiplication facts up to 10 × 10 and using them in multiplication and division problems.

SKILLS

► Multiplying by single-digit numbers
► Dividing by single-digit numbers

APPARATUS

Squared paper

NOTES

Children creating their own multiplying grids, using multiplication in both directions, will find the numbers in the grids soon become large. It is easiest to start with very small numbers.

When using division, the top corner number has to be carefully selected so that it can be divided repeatedly by the same number.

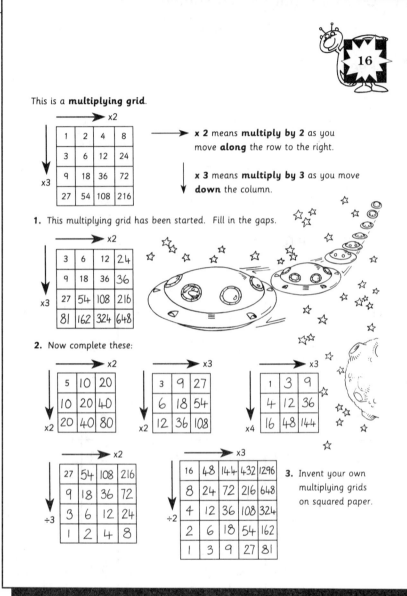

This is a **multiplying grid**.

x2

1	2	4	8
3	6	12	24
9	18	36	72
27	54	108	216

x3

x 2 means **multiply by 2** as you move **along** the row to the right.

x 3 means **multiply by 3** as you move **down** the column.

1. This multiplying grid has been started. Fill in the gaps.

x2

3	6	12	24
9	18	36	36
27	54	108	216
81	162	324	648

x3

2. Now complete these:

x2

5	10	20
10	20	40
20	40	80

x2

x3

3	9	27
6	18	54
12	36	108

x2

x3

1	3	9
4	12	36
16	48	144

x4

x2

27	54	108	216
9	18	36	72
3	6	12	24
1	2	4	8

÷3

x3

16	48	144	432	1296
8	24	72	216	648
4	12	36	108	324
2	6	18	54	162
1	3	9	27	81

÷2

3. Invent your own multiplying grids on squared paper.

SPECTRUM LINKS

	Data Handling	Games	Investigations	Algebra/S&S	Number Skills
Starting					**21** Grids
More					**13** Arrow Grids

Multiplying Grids

This is a **multiplying grid**.

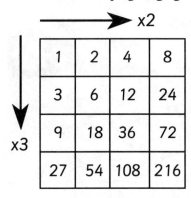

x 2 means **multiply by 2** as you move **along** the row to the right.

x 3 means **multiply by 3** as you move **down** the column.

1. This multiplying grid has been started. Fill in the gaps.

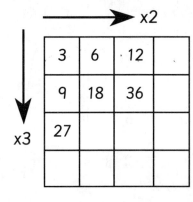

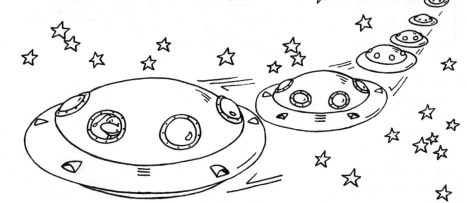

2. Now complete these:

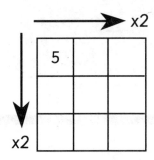

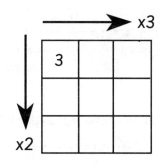

3. Invent your own multiplying grids on squared paper.

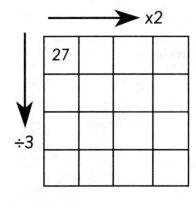

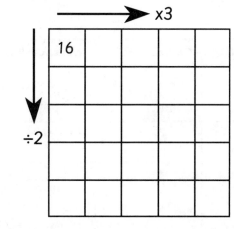

Minus A Digit

LEVEL	UA	N	SSM	HD	A
1					
2		●			
3	●				
4	●	●			
5	●				
6					

● Subtracting two-digit numbers.
● Collecting data to produce a frequency table.

SKILLS
► Subtracting two-digit numbers

NOTE
Children can find out which digit is most often missing by making a frequency table like this:

Digit ｜ 1 2 3 4 5 6 7 8 9
Frequency ｜

1. Find the missing digits in these **subtractions**.
   The digits can be any between 0 and 9.

```
  7 8        5 6        6 7        4 8
- 3 5      - 3 2      - 1 5      - 3 7
 [4][3]     [2] 4      5 [2]      [1][1]

  8 5        7 7        3 [9]      [5] 4
- 4[2]     - [3] 4    - 2 6      - 2 3
 [4] 3      4 [3]      [1] 3      3 [1]

  3 6        5 2        6 4        5 1
- 1 [7]    - [2] 8    - 2 [8]    - [2] 8
 [1] 9      2 [4]      [3] 6      2 [3]

  8 [1]      [5] 4      7 [1]      [4] 4
- 2 9      - 3 8      - 5 5      - 2 9
 [5] 2      1 [6]      [1] 6      1 [5]
```

2. Which digit is most often missing on this page?

3. Invent some of your own missing digit subtraction puzzles, and get a friend to do them.

Question 2: 1 is most often missing.

SPECTRUM LINKS

	Data Handling	Games	Investigations	Algebra/S&S	Number Skills
Starting			17 Totals		
More			25 4-Card Fun		7 What's Missing? 22 Nearly 60 36 Differences
Go Further With					8 Nearly 20 9 5-Card Sums 27 Subtraction Guessing 35 Mixed Totals

Minus A Digit

1. Find the missing digits in these **subtractions**.
The digits can be any between 0 and 9.

```
   7 8        5 6        6 7        4 8
 - 3 5      - 3 2      - 1 5      - 3 7
 ┌─┬─┐      ┌─┐ 4       5 ┌─┐     ┌─┬─┐
 └─┴─┘      └─┘         └─┘       └─┴─┘
```

```
   8 5        7 7        3 ☐        ☐ 4
 - 4 ☐      - ☐ 4      - 2 6      - 2 3
  ☐ 3        4 ☐        ☐ 3        3 ☐
```

```
   3 6        5 2        6 4        5 1
 - 1 ☐      - ☐ 8      - 2 ☐      - ☐ 8
  ☐ 9        2 ☐        ☐ 6        2 ☐
```

```
   8 ☐        ☐ 4        7 ☐        ☐ 4
 - 2 9      - 3 8      - 5 5      - 2 9
  ☐ 2        1 ☐        ☐ 6        1 ☐
```

2. Which digit is most often missing on this page?

3. Invent some of your own missing digit subtraction puzzles,
and get a friend to do them.

Factor Grids

LEVEL	UA	N	SSM	HD	A
1					
2					
3	●				
4	●	●			
5	●				
6					

- ● Learning multiplication facts up to 10 × 10 and using them in multiplication and division problems.
- ● Generalising, mainly in words, patterns, eg, 'factor'.

SKILLS

► Finding factors
► Multiplying by single-digit numbers

NOTES

Children will need to understand what is meant by a 'prime number'.

The activity can lead to exploration of numbers which have many factors. i.e. the numbers which appear in the bottom right-hand corner. So, for example, the factors of 36 are: 1, 2, 3, 4, 6, 9, 12, 18, 36 (36 has nine factors altogether.)

The size of the grid determines the number of factors for the number in the bottom right-hand corner.

This is a **factor grid**. You can use it to find, for example, the **factors** of **18**: 1, 2, 3, 6, 9, 18.

or the factors of **12**: 1, 2, 3, 4, 6, 12.

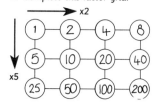

1. Complete this factor grid:

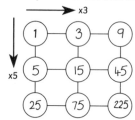

2. Now write the:

factors of **20** 1, 2, 4, 5, 10, 20

factors of **50** 1, 2, 5, 10, 25, 50

factors of **40** 1, 2, 4, 8, 5, 10, 20, 40

factors of **100** 1, 2, 4, 5, 10, 20, 25, 50, 100

3. Complete these and write some lists of factors.

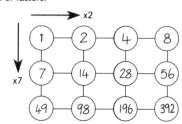

4. Make some more factor grids. You can make them by multiplying numbers in the grid by any pair of **prime numbers** (2, 3, 5, 7, 11, 13 and so on).

SPECTRUM LINKS

	Data Handling	Games	Investigations	Algebra/S&S	Number Skills
More		37 Snake Bite 38 Divido	6 Table Patterns 7 Pick Your Cards 8 Table Ends	8 Completing Rectangles 12 Sift the Multiples 13 Table Patterns	16 Factor Pairs 26 Cloud Numbers
Go Further With		13 Race Track 20 Factor 24 Multiple Choice	9 Factors 13 Tables	4 Prime Numbers 17 Factor Graph 18 Multiplication Machines	11 Lowest Common Multiples 12 Factor Show 25 Highest Common Factors

Factor Grids

This is a **factor grid**.
You can use it to find, for example,
the **factors** of **18**: 1, 2, 3, 6, 9, 18.

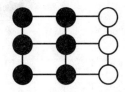

x2

```
  1 — 2 — 4
  |   |   |
  3 — 6 — 12
  |   |   |
x3 9 — 18 — 36
```

or the factors of **12**: 1, 2, 3, 4, 6, 12.

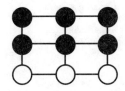

1. Complete this factor grid:

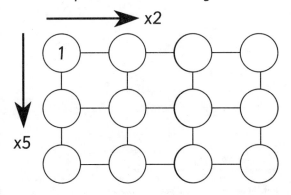

2. Now write the:

factors of **20** _____

factors of **50** _____

factors of **40** _____

factors of **100** _____

3. Complete these and write some lists of factors.

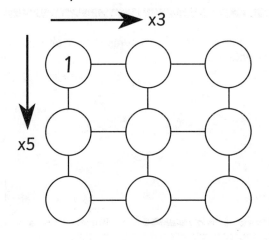

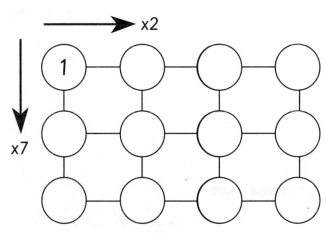

4. Make some more factor grids. You can make them by multiplying numbers in the grid by any pair of **prime numbers** (2, 3, 5, 7, 11, 13 and so on).

Remainder Charts

LEVEL	UA	N	SSM	HD	A
1					
2					
3	●	●			
4	●	●			
5	●				
6					

● Understanding remainders.
● Dividing two-digit numbers by single-digit numbers.

SKILLS

► Dividing by single-digit numbers
► Finding remainders
► Multiplying by single-digit numbers

NOTE

Discuss what it means when '0' appears in a chart.

EXTENSION

► If the 16 remainder chart is extended, for example, from 2 to 16, then all possible remainders can be analysed. This can lead to discussion about which numbers could not appear in this chart and why.

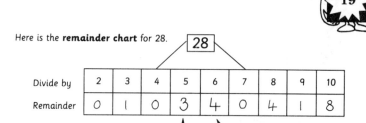

Here is the **remainder chart** for 28.

28

Divide by	2	3	4	5	6	7	8	9	10
Remainder	0	1	0	3	4	0	4	1	8

When 28 is divided by 5, there is a remainder of 3. Write it here.

When 28 is divided by 6, there is a **remainder** of 4. Write it here.

1. Divide 28 by other numbers, and complete the remainder chart. Write about anything you notice. (Hint: think about factors.)

2. Now complete these remainder charts:

24

Divide by	2	3	4	5	6	7	8	9	10
Remainder	0	0	0	4	0	3	0	6	4

16

Divide by	2	3	4	5	6	7	8	9	10
Remainder	0	1	0	1	4	2	0	7	6

35

Divide by	2	3	4	5	6	7	8	9	10
Remainder	1	2	3	0	5	0	3	8	5

3. Make the charts longer to show remainders if you are dividing by numbers greater than 10.

4. Invent some remainder charts of your own.

Question 1: Children should notice that, when a number is divided by one of its factors, the remainder is 0.

SPECTRUM LINKS

	Data Handling	Games	Investigations	Algebra/S&S	Number Skills
Go Further With		**2** Remainders **10** Sixes **27** Sevens **28** Divide It **34** Left Overs	**9** Factors **25** Divisions **40** Remainders	**19** Remainder Tables	

Remainder Charts

Here is the **remainder chart** for 28.

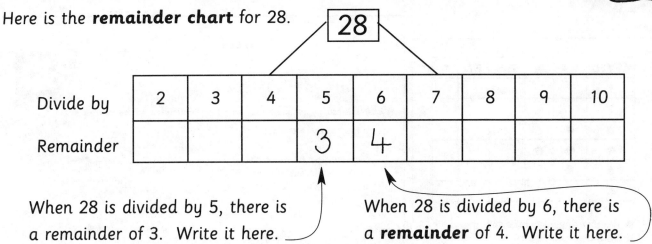

Divide by	2	3	4	5	6	7	8	9	10
Remainder				3	4				

When 28 is divided by 5, there is a remainder of 3. Write it here.

When 28 is divided by 6, there is a **remainder** of 4. Write it here.

1. Divide 28 by other numbers, and complete the remainder chart. Write about anything you notice. (Hint: think about factors.)

2. Now complete these remainder charts:

24

Divide by	2	3	4	5	6	7	8	9	10
Remainder									

16

Divide by	2	3	4	5	6	7	8	9	10
Remainder									

35

Divide by	2	3	4	5	6	7	8	9	10
Remainder									

3. Make the charts longer to show remainders if you are dividing by numbers greater than 10.

4. Invent some remainder charts of your own.

Multiple Percentages

LEVEL	UA	N	SSM	HD	A
1					
2					
3	●				
4	●	●			
5	●				
6					

- ● Recognising and understanding simple percentages.
- ● Multiplication facts.
- ● Multiples.

SKILLS

► Expressing proportion as a percentage
► Recognising multiples of single-digit numbers

APPARATUS

Special Paper 2 for the extensions

NOTE

Ask children to make predictions about the percentages of, for example, the multiples of 5, multiples of 6, multiples of 7, and so on.

EXTENSIONS

► Using Special Paper 2, children can make their own 100 charts and find percentages of other multiples.
► Extend to square numbers, prime numbers, etc. Use Special Paper 2 for this, too.

In this activity you must find two things: **multiples** and **percentages**.

In this 100 chart, the multiples of 2 have been shaded.
There are 50 of them. So, the percentage of numbers which are multiples of 2 is: $\frac{50}{100}$ | 50% |

1. Here the multiples of 2 and 3 have been shaded.
The percentage which are multiples of 2 or 3 is: | 71 |

2. Colour these squares and find the percentages.

Percentage which are multiples of 4 is: | 25 |

Percentage which are multiples of 3 or 4 is: | 50 |

Percentage which are multiples of 7 or 9 is: | 24 |

Percentage which are multiples of 3 or 5 is: | 47 |

SPECTRUM LINKS

	Data Handling	Games	Investigations	Algebra/S&S	Number Skills
More			6 Table Patterns 8 Table Ends	6 Multiple Gaps 12 Sift the Multiples 18 Patterns With 9	16 Factor Pairs 26 Cloud Numbers 33 The Right Boxes
Go Further With	26 Sevens 36 Multiplication Tables	17 Fives and Threes 24 Multiple Choice	13 Tables 37 Multiples	17 Factor Graph	20 Goal Percentages 33 Tridiscs 36 Percentage Wheels

Multiple Percentages

In this activity you must find two things: **multiples** and **percentages**.

In this 100 chart, the multiples of 2 have been shaded.

There are 50 of them. So, the percentage of numbers which are multiples of 2 is: $\dfrac{50}{100}$ $\boxed{50\%}$

1	2	3	4	5	6	7	8	9	10
11	12	13	14	15	16	17	18	19	20
21	22	23	24	25	26	27	28	29	30
31	32	33	34	35	36	37	38	39	40
41	42	43	44	45	46	47	48	49	50
51	52	53	54	55	56	57	58	59	60
61	62	63	64	65	66	67	68	69	70
71	72	73	74	75	76	77	78	79	80
81	82	83	84	85	86	87	88	89	90
91	92	93	94	95	96	97	98	99	100

1. Here the multiples of 2 and 3 have been shaded.
The percentage which are multiples of 2 or 3 is: ☐

1	2	3	4	5	6	7	8	9	10
11	12	13	14	15	16	17	18	19	20
21	22	23	24	25	26	27	28	29	30
31	32	33	34	35	36	37	38	39	40
41	42	43	44	45	46	47	48	49	50
51	52	53	54	55	56	57	58	59	60
61	62	63	64	65	66	67	68	69	70
71	72	73	74	75	76	77	78	79	80
81	82	83	84	85	86	87	88	89	90
91	92	93	94	95	96	97	98	99	100

2. Colour these squares and find the percentages.

1	2	3	4	5	6	7	8	9	10
11	12	13	14	15	16	17	18	19	20
21	22	23	24	25	26	27	28	29	30
31	32	33	34	35	36	37	38	39	40
41	42	43	44	45	46	47	48	49	50
51	52	53	54	55	56	57	58	59	60
61	62	63	64	65	66	67	68	69	70
71	72	73	74	75	76	77	78	79	80
81	82	83	84	85	86	87	88	89	90
91	92	93	94	95	96	97	98	99	100

Percentage which are multiples of 4 is: ☐

1	2	3	4	5	6	7	8	9	10
11	12	13	14	15	16	17	18	19	20
21	22	23	24	25	26	27	28	29	30
31	32	33	34	35	36	37	38	39	40
41	42	43	44	45	46	47	48	49	50
51	52	53	54	55	56	57	58	59	60
61	62	63	64	65	66	67	68	69	70
71	72	73	74	75	76	77	78	79	80
81	82	83	84	85	86	87	88	89	90
91	92	93	94	95	96	97	98	99	100

Percentage which are multiples of 3 or 4 is: ☐

1	2	3	4	5	6	7	8	9	10
11	12	13	14	15	16	17	18	19	20
21	22	23	24	25	26	27	28	29	30
31	32	33	34	35	36	37	38	39	40
41	42	43	44	45	46	47	48	49	50
51	52	53	54	55	56	57	58	59	60
61	62	63	64	65	66	67	68	69	70
71	72	73	74	75	76	77	78	79	80
81	82	83	84	85	86	87	88	89	90
91	92	93	94	95	96	97	98	99	100

Percentage which are multiples of 7 or 9 is: ☐

1	2	3	4	5	6	7	8	9	10
11	12	13	14	15	16	17	18	19	20
21	22	23	24	25	26	27	28	29	30
31	32	33	34	35	36	37	38	39	40
41	42	43	44	45	46	47	48	49	50
51	52	53	54	55	56	57	58	59	60
61	62	63	64	65	66	67	68	69	70
71	72	73	74	75	76	77	78	79	80
81	82	83	84	85	86	87	88	89	90
91	92	93	94	95	96	97	98	99	100

Percentage which are multiples of 3 or 5 is: ☐

SPECTRUM MATHS ■ GO FURTHER WITH NUMBER SKILLS

Division Grids

LEVEL	UA	N	SSM	HD	A
1					
2					
3	●	●			
4	●	●			
5	●				
6					

- Dividing two-digit numbers by single-digit numbers.
- Recognising that multiplication and division are inverse operations.

SKILLS

► Dividing two-digit numbers by single-digit numbers
► Multiplying as the inverse of dividing
► Adding two-digit numbers

NOTE

In order to complete question 2, children may need some help in understanding that multiplication and division are inverse operations.

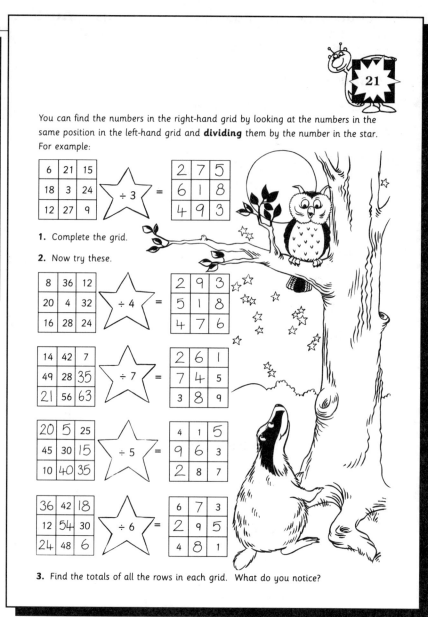

You can find the numbers in the right-hand grid by looking at the numbers in the same position in the left-hand grid and **dividing** them by the number in the star. For example:

6	21	15
18	3	24
12	27	9

÷ 3 =

2	7	5
6	1	8
4	9	3

1. Complete the grid.

2. Now try these.

8	36	12
20	4	32
16	28	24

÷ 4 =

2	9	3
5	1	8
4	7	6

14	42	7
49	28	35
21	56	63

÷ 7 =

2	6	1
7	4	5
3	8	9

20	5	25
45	30	15
10	40	35

÷ 5 =

4	1	5
9	6	3
2	8	7

36	42	18
12	54	30
24	48	6

÷ 6 =

6	7	3
2	9	5
4	8	1

3. Find the totals of all the rows in each grid. What do you notice?

3. The row totals of the left-hand grids, when divided, give the row totals of the right-hand grids.

SPECTRUM LINKS

	Data Handling	Games	Investigations	Algebra/S&S	Number Skills
Starting					**11** Addition Wheels
More		**38** Divido			**21** Multiplication Wheels
Go Further With		**10** Sixes **27** Sevens **28** Divide It	**9** Factors **25** Divisions **40** Remainders	**19** Remainder Tables	**24** Division Wheels

Division Grids

You can find the numbers in the right-hand grid by looking at the numbers in the same position in the left-hand grid and **dividing** them by the number in the star. For example:

6	21	15
18	3	24
12	27	9

÷ 3 =

2	7	5
6		

1. Complete the grid.

2. Now try these.

8	36	12
20	4	32
16	28	24

÷ 4 =

14	42	7
49	28	
	56	

÷ 7 =

		5
3		9

		25
45	30	
10		

÷ 5 =

4	1	
		3
	8	7

	42	
12		30
	48	

÷ 6 =

6		3
	9	
4		1

3. Find the totals of all the rows in each grid. What do you notice?

Place Nine

LEVEL	UA	N	SSM	HD	A
1					
2					
3	●	●			
4	●	●			
5	●				
6					

● Learning and using adding and subtraction facts.
● Adding several single-digit numbers.

SKILLS

► Adding and subtracting
► Seeking arrangements of numbers in a two-way table to match given totals

APPARATUS

Numbered cards, 1-9

NOTES

Ask children to draw a large 3 x 3 grid on paper, and use a set of numbered cards to place in the grid.

They can also make labels to represent the row and column totals, and place these in position for each puzzle.
The task can be made easier by giving children an extra clue (number in a square).

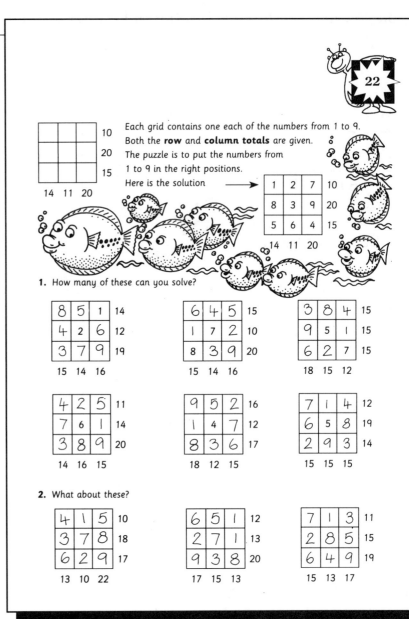

Each grid contains one each of the numbers from 1 to 9.
Both the **row** and **column totals** are given.
The puzzle is to put the numbers from 1 to 9 in the right positions.
Here is the solution →

			10
			20
			15
14 11 20

1	2	7	10
8	3	9	20
5	6	4	15
14 11 20

1. How many of these can you solve?

8	5	1	14
4	2	6	12
3	7	9	19
15 14 16

6	4	5	15
1	7	2	10
8	3	9	20
15 14 16

3	8	4	15
9	5	1	15
6	2	7	15
18 15 12

4	2	5	11
7	6	1	14
3	8	9	20
14 16 15

9	5	2	16
1	4	7	12
8	3	6	17
18 12 15

7	1	4	12
6	5	8	19
2	9	3	14
15 15 15

2. What about these?

4	1	5	10
3	7	8	18
6	2	9	17
13 10 22

6	5	1	12
2	7	1	13
9	3	8	20
17 15 13

7	1	3	11
2	8	5	15
6	4	9	19
15 13 17

SPECTRUM LINKS

	Data Handling	Games	Investigations	Algebra/S&S	Number Skills
More		26 Fifteens			18 2 x 2 Addition Squares 25 Addition Grids 26 Cloud Numbers
Go Further With					2 Magic Squares

Place Nine

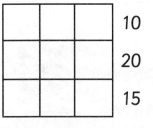

14 11 20

Each grid contains one each of the numbers from 1 to 9.
Both the **row** and **column totals** are given.
The puzzle is to put the numbers from
1 to 9 in the right positions.
Here is the solution ⟶

1	2	7	10
8	3	9	20
5	6	4	15

14 11 20

1. How many of these can you solve?

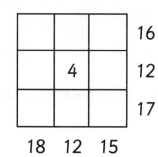

		1	14
	2		12
			19

15 14 16

			15
	7		10
8			20

15 14 16

			15
	5		15
		7	15

18 15 12

			11
	6		14
			20

14 16 15

			16
	4		12
			17

18 12 15

			12
	5		19
			14

15 15 15

2. What about these?

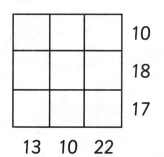

			10
			18
			17

13 10 22

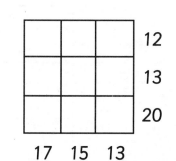

			12
			13
			20

17 15 13

			11
			15
			19

15 13 17

SPECTRUM MATHS ■ GO FURTHER WITH NUMBER SKILLS

Multiples of 10

LEVEL	UA	N	SSM	HD	A
1					
2		●			
3	●	●			
4	●	●			
5	●				
6					

● Addition patterns.
● Number patterns.
● Addition of two-digit numbers.

SKILLS

► Adding sets of numbers to find totals which are multiples of 10

NOTES

Ask the children to look for the sums of units digits which produce multiples of 10. For example, 1 and 9, 2 and 8, 3 and 7, 5 and 5.

This grid contains many strips or groups of numbers whose **total** is a **multiple of 10**.

For example, this strip has a total of 30, which is a multiple of 10.

12
18
30

1	2	3	4	5	6
7	8	9	10	11	12
13	14	15	16	17	18
19	20	21	22	23	24
25	26	27	28	29	30
31	32	33	34	35	36

1. These are the outlines of strips or groups which have numbers whose total is a multiple of 10. See how many you can find. They are all different.

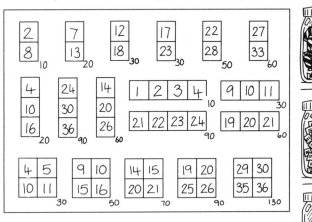

2. See how many strips or groups you can find in this grid with totals which are multiples of 10.

1	2	3	4	5	6	7	8	9	10
11	12	13	14	15	16	17	18	19	20
21	22	23	24	25	26	27	28	29	30

SPECTRUM LINKS

	Data Handling	Games	Investigations	Algebra/S&S	Number Skills
Starting			35 In the Window		4 Giraffe 12 Difference Dog 31 Elephant Tricks
More				19 Unit Digit Patterns	19 Twenties
Go Further With					26 Hexanimals

Multiples of 10

This grid contains many strips or groups of numbers whose **total** is a **multiple of 10**.

For example,
this strip has a total of 30,
which is a multiple of 10.

12
18

30

1	2	3	4	5	6
7	8	9	10	11	12
13	14	15	16	17	18
19	20	21	22	23	24
25	26	27	28	29	30
31	32	33	34	35	36

1. These are the outlines of strips or groups which have numbers whose total is a multiple of 10. See how many you can find. They are all different.

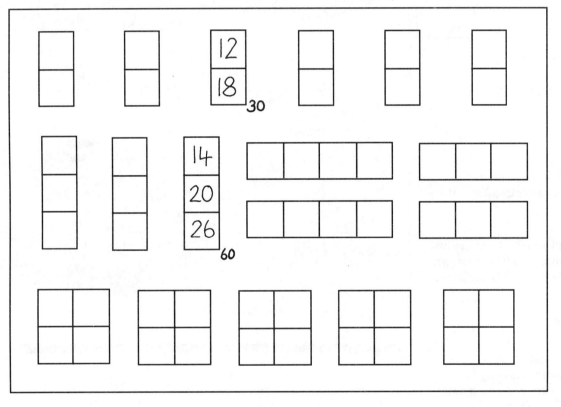

2. See how many strips or groups you can find in this grid with totals which are multiples of 10.

1	2	3	4	5	6	7	8	9	10
11	12	13	14	15	16	17	18	19	20
21	22	23	24	25	26	27	28	29	30

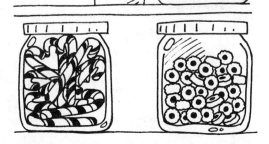

Division Wheels

LEVEL	UA	N	SSM	HD	A
1					
2					
3	●				
4	●	●			
5	●				
6					

- ● Dividing two-digit numbers by a single-digit number.
- ● Recognising that multiplication and division are inverse operations and using this to check calculations.

SKILLS
► Dividing two-digit numbers by single-digit numbers
► Using multiplication as the inverse of division

APPARATUS
Special Paper 3 for the extension activity

NOTE
The table is given as a check. In the first instance, children should be encouraged to try completing the wheels without reference to it.

EXTENSIONS
► Children can build their own division wheels, using Special Paper 3.
► They could take the activity further to include division by numbers greater than 10.

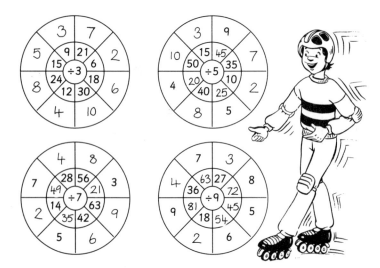

This part of the table shows these **division facts**:
$24 \div 6 = 4$
$24 \div 4 = 6$

1. Write down some more division facts for dividing by 8, and then for dividing by 6.

2. Complete these **division wheels**. The first one has been started for you, to show you how it works. Use the table to check your answers.

x	1	2	3	4	5	6	7	8	9	10
1	1	2	3	4	5	6	7	8	9	10
2	2	4	6	8	10	12	14	16	18	20
3	3	6	9	12	15	18	21	24	27	30
4	4	8	12	16	20	24	28	32	36	40
5	5	10	15	20	25	30	35	40	45	50
6	6	12	18	24	30	36	42	48	54	60
7	7	14	21	28	35	42	49	56	63	70
8	8	16	24	32	40	48	56	64	72	80
9	9	18	27	36	45	54	63	72	81	90
10	10	20	30	40	50	60	70	80	90	100

3. Build your own division wheels using these divisions: ÷ 2, ÷ 4, ÷ 6, ÷ 10

SPECTRUM LINKS

	Data Handling	Games	Investigations	Algebra/S&S	Number Skills
Starting					**11** Addition Wheels
More		**38** Divido			**21** Multiplication Wheels
Go Further With		**10** Sixes **27** Sevens **28** Divide It	**9** Factors **25** Divisions **40** Remainders	**19** Remainder Tables	**21** Division Grids

Division Wheels

This part of the table shows
these **division facts**:
24 ÷ 6 = 4
24 ÷ 4 = 6

1. Write down some more
   division facts for dividing by
   8, and then for dividing by 6.

2. Complete these **division wheels**.
   The first one has been started for you,
   to show you how it works.
   Use the table to check your answers.

x	1	2	3	4	5	6	7	8	9	10
1	1	2	3	4	5	6	7	8	9	10
2	2	4	6	8	10	12	14	16	18	20
3	3	6	9	12	15	18	21	24	27	30
4	4	8	12	16	20	24	28	32	36	40
5	5	10	15	20	25	30	35	40	45	50
6	6	12	18	24	30	36	42	48	54	60
7	7	14	21	28	35	42	49	56	63	70
8	8	16	24	32	40	48	56	64	72	80
9	9	18	27	36	45	54	63	72	81	90
10	10	20	30	40	50	60	70	80	90	100

3. Build your own division wheels using these divisions: ÷ 2, ÷ 4, ÷ 6, ÷ 10

25 Highest Common Factors

LEVEL	UA	N	SSM	HD	A
1					
2					
3	●				
4	●	●			
5	●				
6					

● Division facts.
● Factors.

SKILLS

► Listing the factors of a number
► Finding the highest common factor of two numbers

NOTE

The sheet is best preceded by an activity which involves searching for factors. For example: 18: 'Factor Grids' or 12: 'Factor Show'

On this grid you can show the **highest common** factors of pairs of numbers.
For example:
factors of 12 are: 1, 2, 3, 4, 6, 12
factors of 20 are: 1, 2, 4, 5, 10, 20

Common factors of 12 and 20 are: 1, 2, 4 (that means they are factors of both numbers).
The **highest common factor** of 12 and 20 is: 4

	12	15	8
6	6	3	2
20	4	5	4
16	4	1	8

1. Complete the grid by finding the highest common factors of the other pairs of numbers.

2. Now complete these grids.

	24	16	10
12	12	4	2
15	3	1	5
8	8	8	2

	30	9	32
40	10	1	8
6	6	3	2
18	6	9	2

	30	20	16	36
48	6	4	16	12
10	10	10	2	2
50	10	10	2	2

	32	8	28	14
12	4	4	4	2
18	2	2	2	2
42	2	2	14	7

3. Draw your own grids, and invent your own numbers for finding the highest common factors.

SPECTRUM LINKS

	Data Handling	Games	Investigations	Algebra/S&S	Number Skills
More		37 Snake Bite 38 Divido	6 Table Patterns 7 Pick Your Cards 8 Table Ends	8 Completing Rectangles 12 Sift the Multiples 13 Table Patterns	16 Factor Pairs 26 Cloud Numbers
Go Further With		13 Race Track 20 Factor 24 Multiple Choice	9 Factors 13 Tables	4 Prime Numbers 17 Factor Graph 18 Multiplication Machines	11 Lowest Common Multiples 12 Factor Show 18 Factor Grids

Highest Common Factors

25

On this grid you can show the **highest common** factors of pairs of numbers.

For example:

factors of 12 are: 1, 2, 3, 4, 6, 12

factors of 20 are: 1, 2, 4, 5, 10, 20

Common factors of 12 and 20 are: 1, 2, 4 (that means they are factors of both numbers).

The **highest common factor** of 12 and 20 is: 4

	12	15	8
6			
20	4		
16			

1. Complete the grid by finding the highest common factors of the other pairs of numbers.

2. Now complete these grids.

	24	16	10
12			
15			
8			

	30	9	32
40			
6			
18			

	30	20	16	36
48				
10				
50				

	32	8	28	14
12				
18				
42				

3. Draw your own grids, and invent your own numbers for finding the highest common factors.

Hexanimals

LEVEL	UA	N	SSM	HD	A
1					
2					
3	●	●			
4	●	●			
5	●				
6					

● Learning and using addition and subtraction facts to 20.
● Adding mentally several single-digit numbers.

SKILLS
► Finding sets of several numbers which have a given total

APPARATUS
Special Paper 4, for the initial work and the extension

NOTE
Children can use Special Paper 4 to create their own jungle and to record Hexanimals.

EXTENSION
► Explore different Hexanimals on this grid. For example, start with a total of 10, then 11, then 12, and so on, each time inviting children to find a Hexanimal.

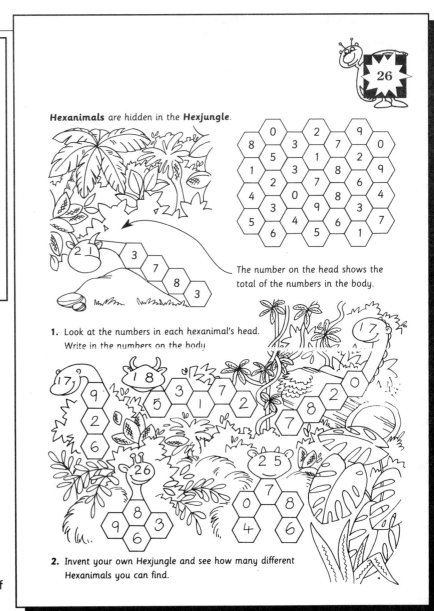

Hexanimals are hidden in the **Hexjungle**.

The number on the head shows the total of the numbers in the body.

1. Look at the numbers in each hexanimal's head. Write in the numbers on the body.

2. Invent your own Hexjungle and see how many different Hexanimals you can find.

SPECTRUM LINKS

	Data Handling	Games	Investigations	Algebra/S&S	Number Skills
Starting			35 In the Window		4 Giraffe 12 Difference Dog 31 Elephant Tricks
More				19 Unit Digit Patterns	19 Twenties
Go Further With					23 Multiples of Ten

Hexanimals

Hexanimals are hidden in the **Hexjungle**.

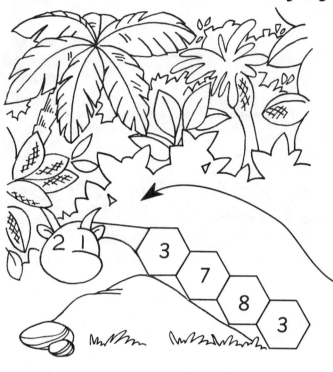

	0		2		9
8		3		7		0
	5		1		2	
1		3		8		9
	2		7		6	
4		0		8		4
	3		9		3	
5		4		6		7
	6		5		1	

The number on the head shows the total of the numbers in the body.

1. Look at the numbers in each hexanimal's head. Write in the numbers on the body.

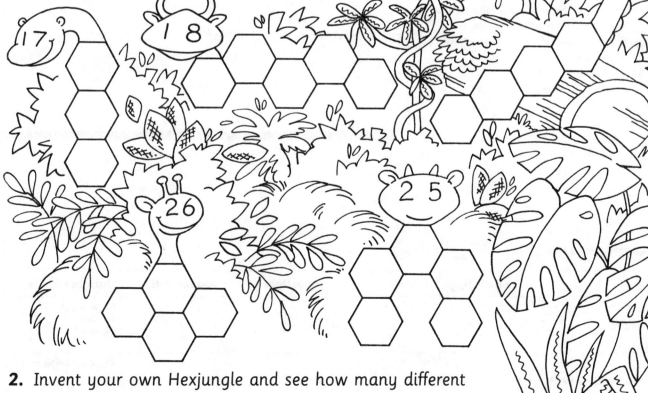

2. Invent your own Hexjungle and see how many different Hexanimals you can find.

SPECTRUM MATHS ■ GO FURTHER WITH NUMBER SKILLS

Subtraction Guessing

LEVEL	UA	N	SSM	HD	A
1					
2					
3	●	●			
4	●	●			
5	●				
6					

- ● Approximating to the nearest 10.
- ● Subtracting two two-digit numbers.
- ● Estimating and approximating to check the validity of subtraction calculations.

SKILLS

- ► Approximating results of subtracting
- ► Rounding numbers to the nearest 10
- ► Using a calculator as a check

APPARATUS

Calculator

EXTENSION

- ► This activity can be extended to much larger numbers which, for example, are rounded off to the nearest 100, e.g.

$$4862 \longrightarrow 5000$$
$$3104 \longrightarrow 3000$$
$$1758 \longleftarrow 2000$$

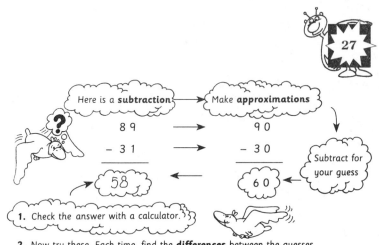

Here is a **subtraction** → Make **approximations**

$$
\begin{array}{r} 8\ 9 \\ -\ 3\ 1 \\ \hline \end{array} \longrightarrow
\begin{array}{r} 9\ 0 \\ -\ 3\ 0 \\ \hline \end{array}
$$

Subtract for your guess

58 ← 60

1. Check the answer with a calculator.

2. Now try these. Each time, find the **differences** between the guesses and the exact answers.

$$
\begin{array}{r} 6\ 2 \to 60 \\ -\ 1\ 8 \to 20 \\ \hline 44 \leftarrow 40 \end{array}
\qquad
\begin{array}{r} 5\ 1 \to 50 \\ -\ 3\ 3 \to 30 \\ \hline 18 \leftarrow 20 \end{array}
\qquad
\begin{array}{r} 8\ 9 \to 90 \\ -\ 5\ 2 \to 50 \\ \hline 37 \leftarrow 40 \end{array}
$$

$$
\begin{array}{r} 6\ 9 \to 70 \\ -\ 3\ 9 \to 40 \\ \hline 30 \leftarrow 30 \end{array}
\qquad
\begin{array}{r} 9\ 1 \to 90 \\ -\ 5\ 8 \to 60 \\ \hline 33 \leftarrow 30 \end{array}
\qquad
\begin{array}{r} 7\ 8 \to 80 \\ -\ 2\ 2 \to 20 \\ \hline 56 \leftarrow 60 \end{array}
$$

3. Now guess the answers to these subtractions, then check with a calculator.

$$
\begin{array}{r} 8\ 7 \\ -\ 7\ 1 \\ \hline \end{array}
\quad
\begin{array}{r} 1\ 2\ 8 \\ -\ \ 6\ 2 \\ \hline \end{array}
\quad
\begin{array}{r} 1\ 3\ 1 \\ -\ \ 7\ 9 \\ \hline \end{array}
\quad
\begin{array}{r} 1\ 0\ 9 \\ -\ \ 4\ 3 \\ \hline \end{array}
\quad
\begin{array}{r} 2\ 0\ 4 \\ -\ 1\ 1\ 9 \\ \hline \end{array}
\quad
\begin{array}{r} 2\ 1\ 1 \\ -\ \ 8\ 7 \\ \hline \end{array}
$$

SPECTRUM LINKS

	Data Handling	Games	Investigations	Algebra/S&S	Number Skills
More					**22** Nearly 60 **36** Differences **40** Which Truck?
Go Further With					**17** Minus a digit

Subtraction Guessing

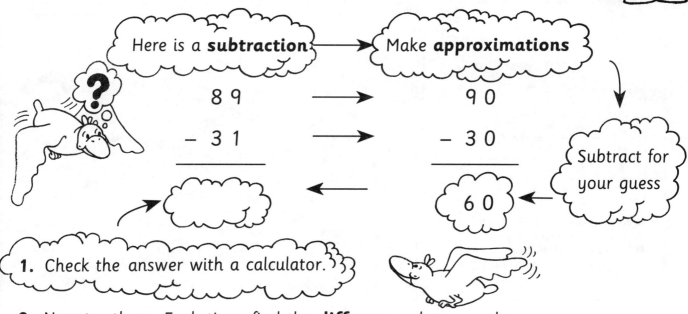

Here is a **subtraction** → Make **approximations**

89 → 90

– 31 → – 30

Subtract for your guess

60

1. Check the answer with a calculator.

2. Now try these. Each time, find the **differences** between the guesses and the exact answers.

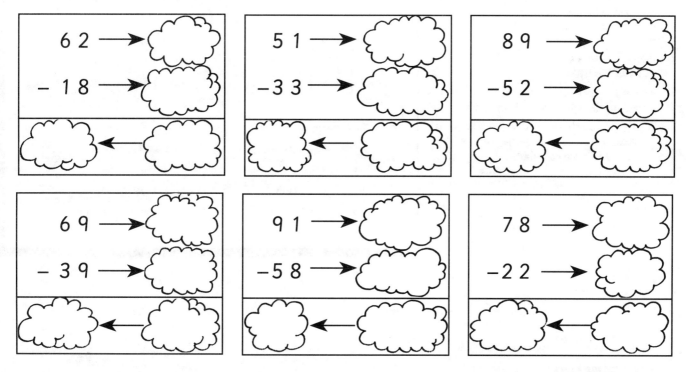

```
  6 2  →
– 1 8  →
```

```
  5 1  →
– 3 3  →
```

```
  8 9  →
– 5 2  →
```

```
  6 9  →
– 3 9  →
```

```
  9 1  →
– 5 8  →
```

```
  7 8  →
– 2 2  →
```

3. Now guess the answers to these subtractions, then check with a calculator.

```
   8 7        1 2 8       1 3 1       1 0 9       2 0 4       2 1 1
 – 7 1      –   6 2     –   7 9     –   4 3     – 1 1 9     –   8 7
 _____     _____     _____     _____     _____     _____
```

SPECTRUM MATHS ■ GO FURTHER WITH NUMBER SKILLS

Goal Percentages

LEVEL	UA	N	SSM	HD	A
1					
2					
3	●	●			
4	●	●			
5	●	●			
6					

- Recognising and understanding simple percentages.
- Calculating percentages.
- Extracting information from tables and lists.

SKILLS

► Expressing proportions of 100, 50 and 25 as a percentage
► Finding percentages of a quantity
► Processing discrete data

EXTENSIONS

► Find percentages when the sets of scores do not total 100, 50 or 25.
► Sunday newspapers provide a range of data, and the percentages can be found using a calculator.

Here is a list of scores for 50 football matches.

H A	H A	H A	H A	H A	H A	H A	H A	H A	H A	H A	H A
0 - 1	0 - 1	1 - 0	1 - 1	4 - 3	5 - 1	2 - 0	1 - 2	0 - 2	0 - 2	1 - 0	0 - 3
1 - 2	0 - 0	3 - 1	6 - 1	0 - 1	0 - 1	4 - 3	1 - 0	1 - 0	3 - 4	1 - 1	2 - 0
2 - 0	1 - 2	0 - 0	1 - 0	0 - 3	1 - 0	3 - 0	0 - 3	2 - 0	1 - 0	0 - 1	0 - 1
1 - 2	2 - 2	1 - 2	1 - 2	1 - 0	1 - 1	5 - 0	1 - 1	1 - 1	0 - 2	1 - 0	1 - 0
1 - 3	1 - 0										

Out of 100 teams, three scored 4 goals.

So the percentage of teams scoring 4 goals is: $\boxed{3\%}$

1. Find these percentages:

Teams scoring 0 goals $\boxed{33\%}$ Teams scoring 2 or more goals $\boxed{30\%}$

Teams scoring 1 goal $\boxed{37\%}$ Matches ending in a draw $\boxed{16\%}$

Teams scoring 2 goals $\boxed{15\%}$ Matches ending in a home win $\boxed{44\%}$

Teams scoring 3 goals $\boxed{9\%}$ Matches ending in an away win $\boxed{40\%}$

Here is a list of the scores in 25 hockey matches:

H A	H A	H A	H A	H A	H A	H A	H A
1 - 0	3 - 1	2 - 0	1 - 1	0 - 0	1 - 4	5 - 0	2 - 1
2 - 0	3 - 3	1 - 1	4 - 1	2 - 3	1 - 1	2 - 1	1 - 2
0 - 1	3 - 1	1 - 0	1 - 1	2 - 1	1 - 6	4 - 4	
4 - 2	2 - 4						

2. Find these percentages:

Teams scoring 0 goals $\boxed{16\%}$ Teams scoring 2 or more goals $\boxed{44\%}$

Teams scoring 1 goal $\boxed{40\%}$ Matches ending in a draw $\boxed{28\%}$

Teams scoring 2 goals $\boxed{18\%}$ Matches ending in a home win $\boxed{48\%}$

Teams scoring 3 goals $\boxed{10\%}$ Matches ending in an away win $\boxed{24\%}$

SPECTRUM LINKS

	Data Handling	Games	Investigations	Algebra/S&S	Number Skills
More	18 Arsenal v Liverpool				
Go Further With					20 Multiple Percentages 33 Tridiscs 36 Percentage Wheels

Goal Percentages

Here is a list of scores for 50 football matches.

H - A	H - A	H - A	H - A	H - A	H - A	H - A	H - A	H - A	H - A	H - A	H - A
0 - 1	0 - 1	1 - 0	1 - 1	4 - 3	5 - 1	2 - 0	1 - 2	0 - 2	0 - 2	1 - 0	0 - 3
1 - 2	0 - 0	3 - 1	6 - 1	0 - 1	0 - 1	4 - 3	1 - 0	1 - 0	3 - 4	1 - 1	2 - 0
2 - 0	1 - 2	0 - 0	1 - 0	0 - 3	1 - 0	3 - 0	0 - 3	2 - 0	1 - 0	0 - 1	0 - 1
1 - 2	2 - 2	1 - 2	1 - 2	1 - 0	1 - 1	5 - 0	1 - 1	1 - 1	0 - 2	1 - 0	1 - 0
1 - 3	1 - 0										

Out of 100 teams, three scored 4 goals.

So the percentage of teams scoring 4 goals is: $\boxed{3\%}$

1. Find these percentages:

Teams scoring 0 goals ☐   Teams scoring 2 or more goals ☐

Teams scoring 1 goal ☐   Matches ending in a draw ☐

Teams scoring 2 goals ☐   Matches ending in a home win ☐

Teams scoring 3 goals ☐   Matches ending in an away win ☐

Here is a list of the scores in 25 hockey matches:

H - A	H - A	H - A	H - A	H - A	H - A	H - A	H - A
1 - 0	3 - 1	2 - 0	1 - 1	0 - 0	1 - 4	5 - 0	2 - 1
2 - 0	3 - 3	1 - 1	4 - 1	2 - 3	1 - 1	2 - 1	1 - 2
0 - 1	3 - 1	1 - 0	1 - 1	2 - 1	1 - 6	4 - 4	
4 - 2	2 - 4						

2. Find these percentages:

Teams scoring 0 goals ☐   Teams scoring 2 or more goals ☐

Teams scoring 1 goal ☐   Matches ending in a draw ☐

Teams scoring 2 goals ☐   Matches ending in a home win ☐

Teams scoring 3 goals ☐   Matches ending in an away win ☐

Consecutive Flowers

LEVEL	UA	N	SSM	HD	A
1					
2					
3	●	●			
4	●	●			
5	●				
6					

● Addition of several numbers.
● Number patterns.
● Generalising patterns in numbers.

SKILLS

► Finding a set of consecutive whole numbers which have a given total
► Approximating by division

NOTE

A useful starting technique is to locate approximate size of the numbers by dividing the centre number by the number of petals.

Consecutive flowers have **consecutive numbers** on the petals, with the total in the centre.

1. Complete these flowers, by writing the numbers on the petals.

2. Invent some more consecutive flowers.

3. What can you say about the totals of flowers with 3 petals?

4. What can you say about the totals of flowers with 5 petals?

Question 3: flowers with 3 petals have centre numbers which are multiples of 3.
Question 4: flowers with 5 petals have centre numbers which are multiples of 5.

SPECTRUM LINKS

	Data Handling	Games	Investigations	Algebra/S&S	Number Skills
Starting					**2** Lucky Number Sweets
More			**21** Three in a Row		**6** Consecutive Trains

Consecutive Flowers

Consecutive flowers have **consecutive numbers** on the petals, with the total in the centre.

1. Complete these flowers, by writing the numbers on the petals.

2. Invent some more consecutive flowers.

3. What can you say about the totals of flowers with 3 petals?

4. What can you say about the totals of flowers with 5 petals?

Fraction Wheels

LEVEL	UA	N	SSM	HD	A
1					
2					
3	●	●			
4	●	●			
5	●	●			
6					

● Recognising and understanding simple fractions.
● Calculating fractions of quantities.

SKILLS

► Writing fractions of a quantity

EXTENSION

► A reverse form of this activity is to provide children with all the numbers in the boxes, and invite them to write the appropriate fraction on each arm.

The number or amount in the centre of each **fraction wheel** can be divided into fractions. The fractions are written on the spokes of the wheel.

1. Write the **fractions** of the centre numbers in the boxes.
   Two have been done for you.

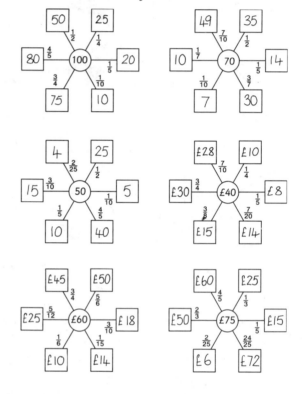

2. Invent your own fraction wheels.

SPECTRUM LINKS

	Data Handling	Games	Investigations	Algebra/S&S	Number Skills
Starting					**38** Colouring Fractions
More		**28** Wheels		**14** Equivalent Fractions	**8** Fraction Shades
Go Further With					**31** Fractions and Decimals **33** Tridiscs

Fraction Wheels

The number or amount in the centre of each **fraction wheel** can be divided into fractions. The fractions are written on the spokes of the wheel.

1. Write the **fractions** of the centre numbers in the boxes.
Two have been done for you.

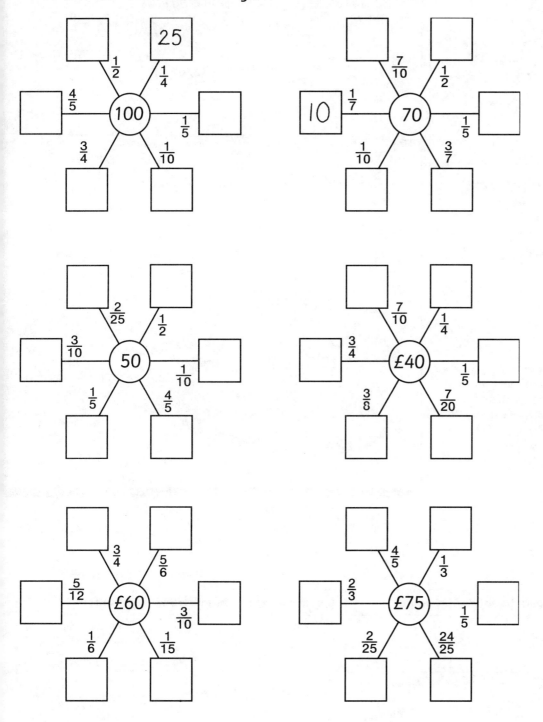

2. Invent your own fraction wheels.

Fractions and Decimals

LEVEL	UA	N	SSM	HD	A
1					
2					
3	●				
4	●				
5	●				
6		●			

● Converting fractions to decimals.

SKILLS

► Equating fractions to decimals
► Creating equivalent fractions and decimals with a given set of digits

APPARATUS

Numbered cards, 0-10

NOTES

Children could start by drawing a large outline of the boxes on a sheet of paper, then select the relevant numbered cards for each problem. Let them explore arrangements of the cards until they find a correct solution. A calculator can be used to check different arrangements.

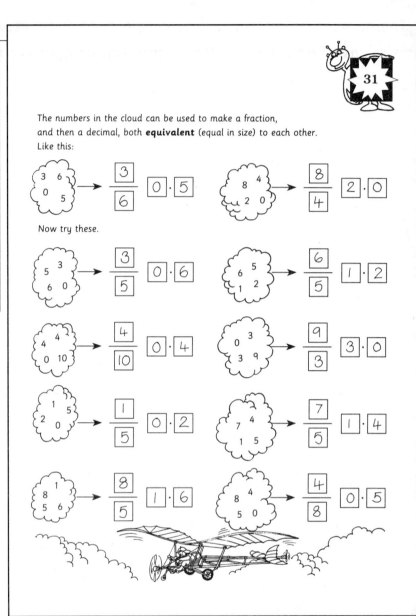

The numbers in the cloud can be used to make a fraction, and then a decimal, both **equivalent** (equal in size) to each other. Like this:

Now try these.

SPECTRUM LINKS

	Data Handling	Games	Investigations	Algebra/S&S	Number Skills
Starting					38 Colouring Fractions
More		28 Wheels		14 Equivalent Fractions	8 Fraction Shades 27 Nearest 100
Go Further With	9 Inches and Centimetres 18 Miles and Kilometres	12 Decimate 14 Two Places 37 Four Rounds	20 Nearest Wholes		39 Decimal Pyramids

Fractions and Decimals

31

The numbers in the cloud can be used to make a fraction,
and then a decimal, both **equivalent** (equal in size) to each other.
Like this:

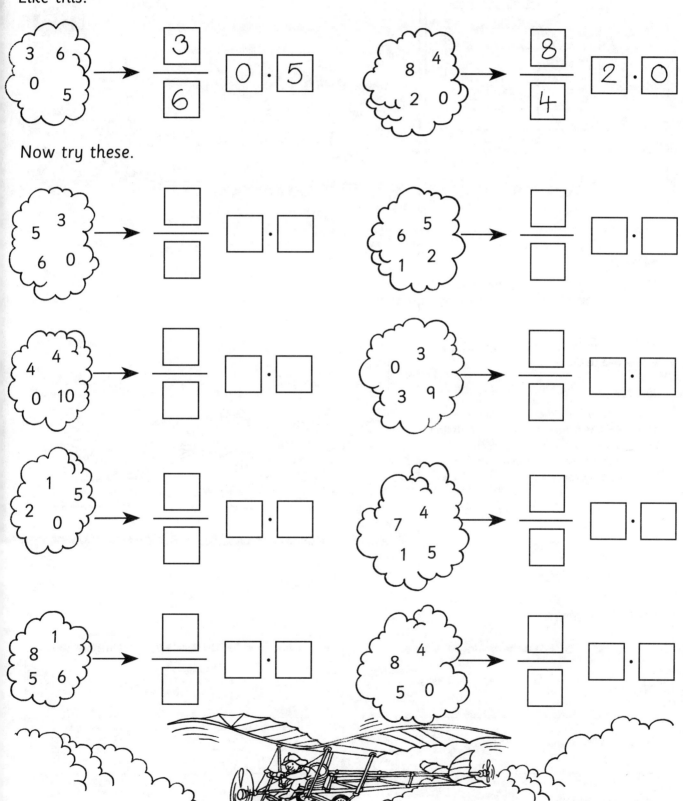

Now try these.

One Hundred

LEVEL	UA	N	SSM	HD	A
1					
2					
3	●	●			
4	●	●			
5	●				
6					

● Addition and subtraction.

SKILLS

► Adding and subtracting, involving single-digit, two-digit and three-digit numbers
► Combining several operations, searching for an arrangement which gives a particular result

NOTE

One strategy to finding a solution is to start with the largest numbers in each line and work down towards the smallest, making adjustments to the use of + and – signs, as you progress.

Each line uses the digits 1 to 9, in order to make **100**. The missing signs are either + or – .

1. Write the missing signs. One has been done for you.

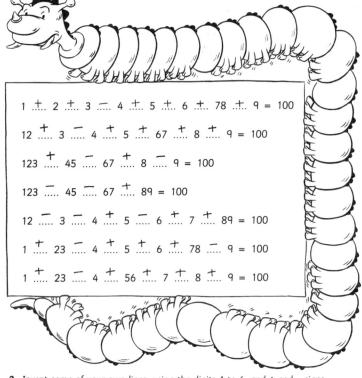

$$1 \underset{+}{...} 2 \underset{+}{...} 3 \underset{-}{...} 4 \underset{+}{...} 5 \underset{+}{...} 6 \underset{+}{...} 78 \underset{+}{...} 9 = 100$$

$$12 \underset{+}{...} 3 \underset{-}{...} 4 \underset{+}{...} 5 \underset{+}{...} 67 \underset{+}{...} 8 \underset{+}{...} 9 = 100$$

$$123 \underset{+}{...} 45 \underset{-}{...} 67 \underset{+}{...} 8 \underset{-}{...} 9 = 100$$

$$123 \underset{-}{...} 45 \underset{-}{...} 67 \underset{+}{...} 89 = 100$$

$$12 \underset{-}{...} 3 \underset{-}{...} 4 \underset{+}{...} 5 \underset{-}{...} 6 \underset{+}{...} 7 \underset{+}{...} 89 = 100$$

$$1 \underset{+}{...} 23 \underset{-}{...} 4 \underset{+}{...} 5 \underset{+}{...} 6 \underset{+}{...} 78 \underset{-}{...} 9 = 100$$

$$1 \underset{+}{...} 23 \underset{-}{...} 4 \underset{+}{...} 56 \underset{+}{...} 7 \underset{+}{...} 8 \underset{+}{...} 9 = 100$$

2. Invent some of your own lines, using the digits 1 to 6, and **+** and **–** signs, to make different answers. Test them out on a friend, with the signs missing.

SPECTRUM LINKS

	Data Handling	Games	Investigations	Algebra/S&S	Number Skills
Starting		**13** Big Match **18** Summary **27** Choosy	**10** Trios **12** Keep Your Balance **14** Card Tricks	**6** Shape Search **10** Stroking Cats **15** Hunt the Numbers	
More		**3** Boxer **8** Dice Superstars	**29** Asking Questions	**10** Mystery People	**15** Dice Lines **20** Equation Solving **28** Arch Numbers **31** Target Practice
Go Further With		**8** A Mouthful **33** Challenge **38** Switch	**16** Number Nine **21** Equations **33** Signs	**7** Number Tricks **10** Think of a Number **14** Whodunnit?	**6** Countdown **13** Three Stones **15** A Special Date

One Hundred

Each line uses the digits 1 to 9, in order to make **100**.
The missing signs are either **+** or **−** .

1. Write the missing signs. One has been done for you.

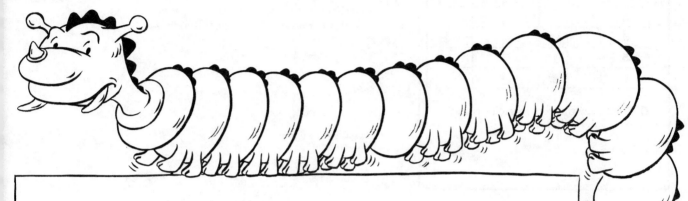

1 ..+.. 2 ..+.. 3 ..−.. 4 ..+.. 5 ..+.. 6 ..+.. 78 ..+.. 9 = 100

12 ..... 3 ..... 4 ..... 5 ..... 67 ..... 8 ..... 9 = 100

123 ..... 45 ..... 67 ..... 8 ..... 9 = 100

123 ..... 45 ..... 67 ..... 89 = 100

12 ..... 3 ..... 4 ..... 5 ..... 6 ..... 7 ..... 89 = 100

1 ..... 23 ..... 4 ..... 5 ..... 6 ..... 78 ..... 9 = 100

1 ..... 23 ..... 4 ..... 56 ..... 7 ..... 8 ..... 9 = 100

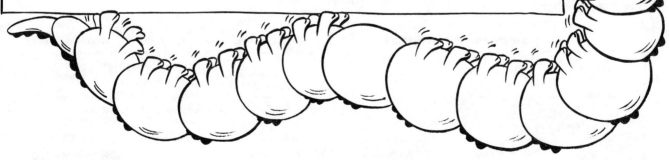

2. Invent some of your own lines, using the digits 1 to 6, and **+** and **−** signs,
to make different answers. Test them out on a friend, with the signs missing.

Tridiscs

LEVEL	UA	N	SSM	HD	A
1					
2					
3					
4					
5					
6		●			

● Converting fractions to decimals and percentages.

SKILLS

► Expressing the equivalence of a fraction, a decimal and a percentage, when given one of them

NOTE

The activity can promote discussion about different possible solutions to the fraction parts e.g. $\frac{2}{5}$ or $\frac{4}{10}$.

Tridiscs contain a percentage, a fraction and a decimal, all of which are **equivalent** to each other. Here are two:

1. Complete these tridiscs:

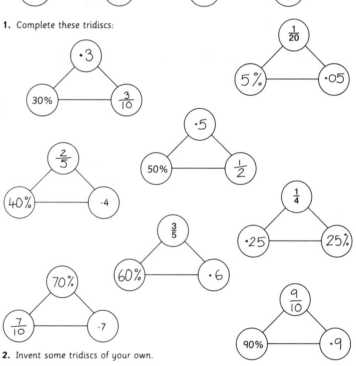

2. Invent some tridiscs of your own.

SPECTRUM LINKS

	Data Handling	Games	Investigations	Algebra/S&S	Number Skills
Starting					38 Colouring Fractions
More		28 Wheels		14 Equivalent Fractions	8 Fraction Shades 27 Nearest 100
Go Further With	9 Inches and Centimetres 18 Miles and Kilometres	12 Decimate 14 Two Places 37 Four Rounds	20 Nearest Wholes		28 Goal Percentages 31 Fractions and Decimals 36 Percentage Wheels 39 Decimal Pyramids

Tridiscs

Tridiscs contain a percentage, a fraction and a decimal,
all of which are **equivalent** to each other. Here are two:

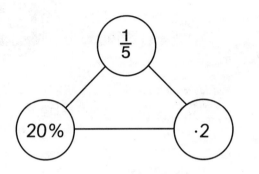

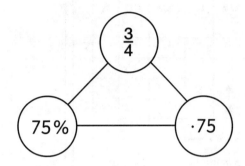

1. Complete these tridiscs:

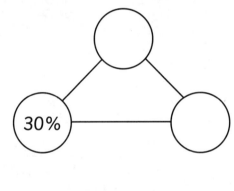

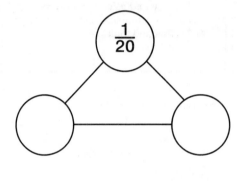

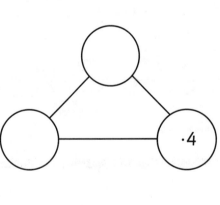

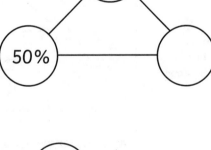

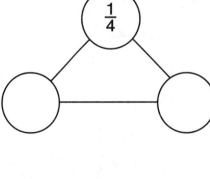

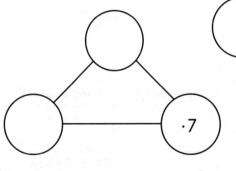

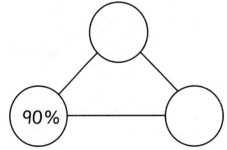

2. Invent some tridiscs of your own.

SPECTRUM MATHS ■ GO FURTHER WITH NUMBER SKILLS

Multiplication Triangles

LEVEL	UA	N	SSM	HD	A
1					
2					
3	●				
4	●	●			
5	●				
6					

● Learning multiplication facts up to 10 × 10 and using them in multiplication and division problems.
● Factors and multiples.

SKILLS

► Multiplying single-digit numbers
► Recognising factors and multiples of numbers
► Using common factors

APPARATUS

Special Paper 5

NOTES

The first group of three are all straightforward and the next can be found by deduction. The last three are best solved by looking for common factors. Children can use Special Paper 5 when they make their own multiplication triangles.

EXTENSION

A further possibility is to make multiplication squares.

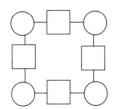

SPECTRUM LINKS

	Data Handling	Games	Investigations	Algebra/S&S	Number Skills
More					**24** Triangle Sums
Go Further With					**14** Number Puzzles

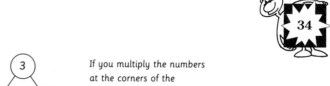

If you multiply the numbers at the corners of the **multiplication triangles**, you get the numbers in the squares. Like this ⟶

7 — 14 — 2

7 x 2 = 14

1. Complete these multiplication triangles.

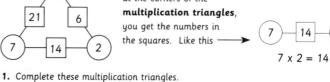

2. Now try these.

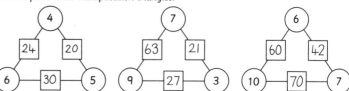

3. And these.

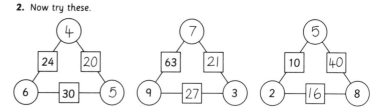

4. Invent some of your own multiplication triangles.

Multiplication Triangles

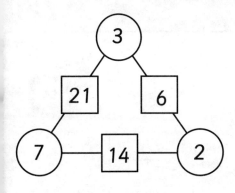

If you multiply the numbers at the corners of the **multiplication triangles**, you get the numbers in the squares. Like this ——▶

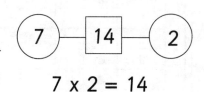

7 x 2 = 14

1. Complete these multiplication triangles.

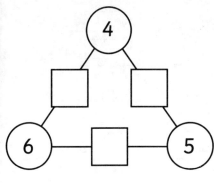   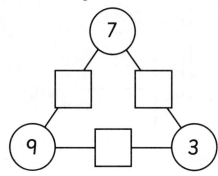   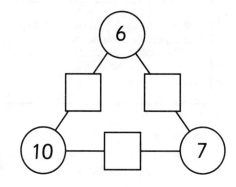

2. Now try these.

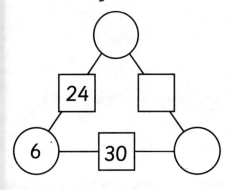   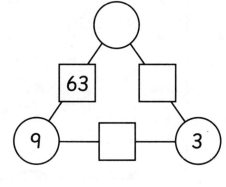   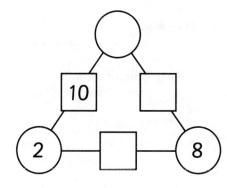

3. And these.

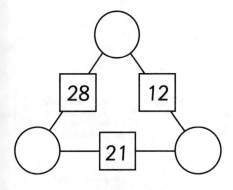   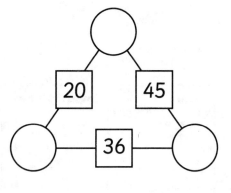   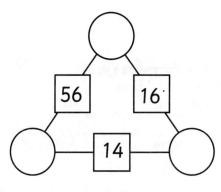

4. Invent some of your own multiplication triangles.

SPECTRUM MATHS ■ GO FURTHER WITH NUMBER SKILLS

35 Mixed Totals

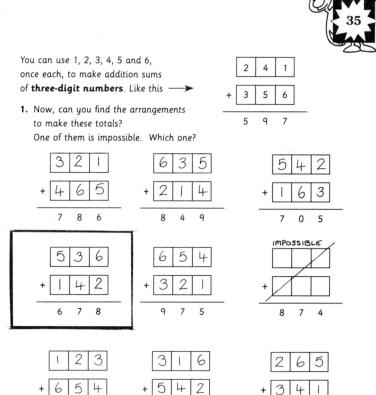

You can use 1, 2, 3, 4, 5 and 6, once each, to make addition sums of **three-digit numbers**. Like this ⟶

```
  2 4 1
+ 3 5 6
-------
  5 9 7
```

1. Now, can you find the arrangements to make these totals?
   One of them is impossible. Which one?

```
  3 2 1        6 3 5        5 4 2
+ 4 6 5      + 2 1 4      + 1 6 3
-------      -------      -------
  7 8 6        8 4 9        7 0 5
```

```
  5 3 6        6 5 4      IMPOSSIBLE
+ 1 4 2      + 3 2 1      +
-------      -------      -------
  6 7 8        9 7 5        8 7 4
```

```
  1 2 3        3 1 6        2 6 5
+ 6 5 4      + 5 4 2      + 3 4 1
-------      -------      -------
  7 7 7        8 5 8        6 0 6
```

2. Can you make any other totals using the numbers 1 to 6 in this way?

LEVEL	UA	N	SSM	HD	A
1					
2					
3	●				
4	●	●			
5	●				
6					

- Adding two three-digit numbers.
- Approximating to check the validity of addition calculations.

SKILLS

► Adding two three-digit numbers without a calculator

APPARATUS

Numbered cards, 1-6

NOTES

Start by drawing a large outline of the three-digit addition. Then use different arrangements of the numbered cards to experiment for different totals.

EXTENSION

► Explore different possible answers for subtraction instead of addition.

SPECTRUM LINKS

	Data Handling	Games	Investigations	Algebra/S&S	Number Skills
More					**22** Nearly 60 **36** Differences
Go Further With					**17** Minus a Digit **27** Subtraction Guessing

Mixed Totals

You can use 1, 2, 3, 4, 5 and 6, once each, to make addition sums of **three-digit numbers**. Like this ⟶

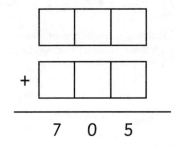

```
  2  4  1
+ 3  5  6
─────────
  5  9  7
```

1. Now, can you find the arrangements to make these totals?
   One of them is impossible.   Which one?

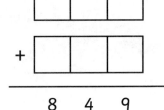

```
 ┌──┬──┬──┐
 │  │  │  │
 └──┴──┴──┘
   ┌──┬──┬──┐
 + │  │  │  │
   └──┴──┴──┘
 ──────────
    7  8  6
```

```
 ┌──┬──┬──┐
 │  │  │  │
 └──┴──┴──┘
   ┌──┬──┬──┐
 + │  │  │  │
   └──┴──┴──┘
 ──────────
    8  4  9
```

```
 ┌──┬──┬──┐
 │  │  │  │
 └──┴──┴──┘
   ┌──┬──┬──┐
 + │  │  │  │
   └──┴──┴──┘
 ──────────
    7  0  5
```

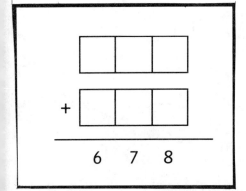

```
 ┌──┬──┬──┐
 │  │  │  │
 └──┴──┴──┘
   ┌──┬──┬──┐
 + │  │  │  │
   └──┴──┴──┘
 ──────────
    6  7  8
```

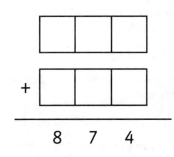

```
 ┌──┬──┬──┐
 │  │  │  │
 └──┴──┴──┘
   ┌──┬──┬──┐
 + │  │  │  │
   └──┴──┴──┘
 ──────────
    9  7  5
```

```
 ┌──┬──┬──┐
 │  │  │  │
 └──┴──┴──┘
   ┌──┬──┬──┐
 + │  │  │  │
   └──┴──┴──┘
 ──────────
    8  7  4
```

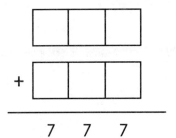

```
 ┌──┬──┬──┐
 │  │  │  │
 └──┴──┴──┘
   ┌──┬──┬──┐
 + │  │  │  │
   └──┴──┴──┘
 ──────────
    7  7  7
```

```
 ┌──┬──┬──┐
 │  │  │  │
 └──┴──┴──┘
   ┌──┬──┬──┐
 + │  │  │  │
   └──┴──┴──┘
 ──────────
    8  5  8
```

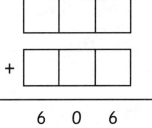

```
 ┌──┬──┬──┐
 │  │  │  │
 └──┴──┴──┘
   ┌──┬──┬──┐
 + │  │  │  │
   └──┴──┴──┘
 ──────────
    6  0  6
```

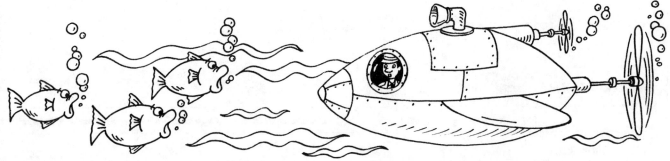

2. Can you make any other totals using the numbers 1 to 6 in this way?

Percentage Wheels

LEVEL	UA	N	SSM	HD	A
1					
2					
3	●				
4	●				
5	●	●			
6		●			

● Calculating percentages of a quantity.
● Finding one number as a percentage of another.

SKILLS

► Finding the percentage of a quantity
► Expressing one quantity as a percentage of another

APPARATUS

Special Paper 6 for the initial activity and the extension

NOTE

Children can use Special Paper 6 when they invent their own wheels.

EXTENSION

► Try reversing the process: make some wheels with all the boxes filled and ask the children to find the percentages to write on the spokes.

There is a number in the **hub** of each wheel and a **percentage** on each **spoke**. Use these to work out which number goes in the box.

1. Write the percentages of the centre number in the boxes.
   Two have been done for you.

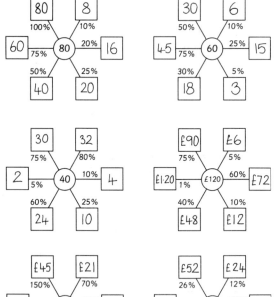

2. Invent your own percentage wheels and ask a friend to fill in the boxes.
   (Work out the answers for yourself, first.)

SPECTRUM LINKS

	Data Handling	Games	Investigations	Algebra/S&S	Number Skills
Go Further With					20 Multiple Percentages 28 Goal Percentages

Percentage Wheels

There is a number in the **hub** of each wheel and a **percentage** on each **spoke**.
Use these to work out which number goes in the box.

1. Write the percentages of the centre number in the boxes.
Two have been done for you.

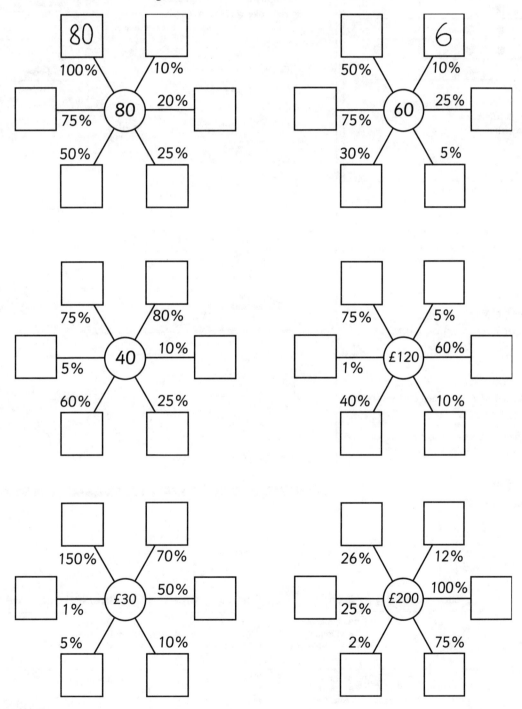

2. Invent your own percentage wheels and ask a friend to fill in the boxes.
(Work out the answers for yourself, first.)

Five Ways

LEVEL	UA	N	SSM	HD	A
1					
2					
3	●				
4	●	●			
5	●	●			●
6					

- Addition, subtraction, multiplication and division.
- Simple equations.

SKILLS

► Writing expressions for numbers using combinations of addition, subtraction, multiplication and division
► Using brackets

APPARATUS

Special Paper 7 for question 2 and the extension

NOTES

The activity can promote discussion about the need for brackets.

Special Paper 7 can be used for finding 'five ways' with some other numbers.

EXTENSION

► Vary the original five numbers.

Use the digits 1, 3, 4, 7 and 8, only.
Here are **five ways** of making 20 ⟶
Each number can only appear once on a line.

20
$1 + 4 + 7 + 8$
$(4 \times 7) - 8$
$8 + (3 \times 4)$
$13 + 7$
$31 - 4 - 7$

1. Can you find five ways of making these?

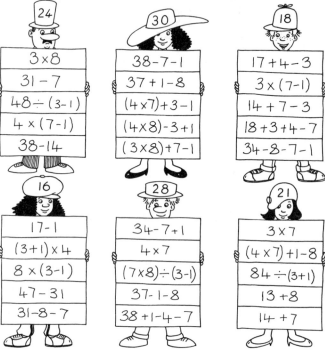

24
3×8
$31 - 7$
$48 \div (3-1)$
$4 \times (7-1)$
$38 - 14$

30
$38 - 7 - 1$
$37 + 1 - 8$
$(4 \times 7) + 3 - 1$
$(4 \times 8) - 3 + 1$
$(3 \times 8) + 7 - 1$

18
$17 + 4 - 3$
$3 \times (7-1)$
$14 + 7 - 3$
$18 + 3 + 4 - 7$
$34 - 8 - 7 - 1$

16
$17 - 1$
$(3+1) \times 4$
$8 \times (3-1)$
$47 - 31$
$31 - 8 - 7$

28
$34 - 7 + 1$
4×7
$(7 \times 8) \div (3-1)$
$37 - 1 - 8$
$38 + 1 - 4 - 7$

21
3×7
$(4 \times 7) + 1 - 8$
$84 \div (3+1)$
$13 + 8$
$14 + 7$

2. See if you can find five ways of making some other numbers.

SPECTRUM LINKS

	Data Handling	Games	Investigations	Algebra/S&S	Number Skills
Starting		13 Big Match 18 Summary 27 Choosy	10 Trios 12 Keep Your Balance 14 Card Tricks	6 Shape Search 10 Stroking Cats 15 Hunt the Numbers	
More		3 Boxer 8 Dice Superstars	29 Asking Questions	10 Mystery People	15 Dice Lines 20 Equation Solving 28 Arch Numbers 31 Target Practice
Go Further With		8 A Mouthful 33 Challenge 38 Switch	16 Number Nine 21 Equations 33 Signs	10 Think of a Number 14 Whodunnit? 7 Number Tricks	6 Countdown 7 Mixed Equations 13 Three Stones

Five Ways

Use the digits 1, 3, 4, 7 and 8, only.
Here are **five ways** of making 20 ⟶
Each number can only appear once on a line.

| 1 + 4 + 7 + 8 |
| (4 x 7) – 8 |
| 8 + (3 x 4) |
| 13 + 7 |
| 31 – 4 – 7 |

1. Can you find five ways of making these?

2. See if you can find five ways of making some other numbers.

Take Your Pick

LEVEL	UA	N	SSM	HD	A
1					
2					
3					
4					
5		●			
6					

● Multiplying single-digit numbers of powers of 10.

SKILLS

► Estimating the result of multiplying together two numbers which are multiples of 10

APPARATUS

Calculator

NOTES

Accurate multiplication can first be attempted without a calculator, then checked with a calculator.

EXTENSIONS

► Ask children to produce two multiples of 10 which have a given product, such as 1800.
► Explore the different ways of reaching the same product, such as:
20 x 90, 30 x 60

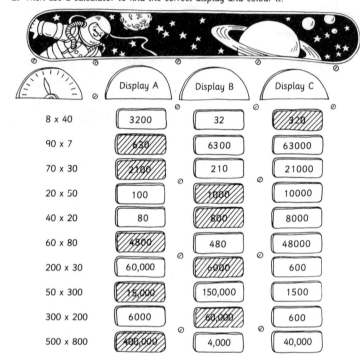

The answer to each multiplication is on **display A**, **display B** or **display C**.

1. Guess the answer to each multiplication by ticking one of the displays.

2. Then use a calculator to find the correct display and colour it.

	Display A	Display B	Display C
8 x 40	3200	32	320
90 x 7	630	6300	63000
70 x 30	2100	210	21000
20 x 50	100	1000	10000
40 x 20	80	800	8000
60 x 80	4800	480	48000
200 x 30	60,000	6000	600
50 x 300	15,000	150,000	1500
300 x 200	6000	60,000	600
500 x 800	400,000	4,000	40,000

3. Write down ten more multiplications involving multiples of 10.

4. Guess the answers, then check with calculator.

SPECTRUM LINKS

	Data Handling	Games	Investigations	Algebra/S&S	Number Skills
More					40 Which Truck?

Take Your Pick

The answer to each multiplication is on **display A**, **display B** or **display C**.

1. Guess the answer to each multiplication by ticking one of the displays.

2. Then use a calculator to find the correct display and colour it.

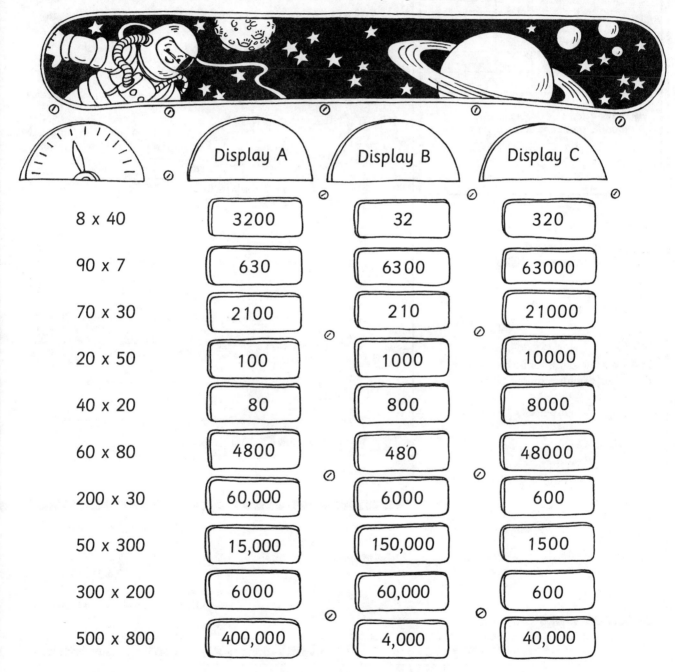

	Display A	Display B	Display C
8 x 40	3200	32	320
90 x 7	630	6300	63000
70 x 30	2100	210	21000
20 x 50	100	1000	10000
40 x 20	80	800	8000
60 x 80	4800	480	48000
200 x 30	60,000	6000	600
50 x 300	15,000	150,000	1500
300 x 200	6000	60,000	600
500 x 800	400,000	4,000	40,000

3. Write down ten more multiplications involving multiples of 10.

4. Guess the answers, then check with calculator.

SPECTRUM MATHS ■ GO FURTHER WITH NUMBER SKILLS

Decimal Pyramids

LEVEL	UA	N	SSM	HD	A
1					
2					
3	●				
4	●	●			
5	●				
6					

● Solving addition problems using numbers with one decimal place.

SKILLS

► Adding two decimal numbers each containing one decimal place

APPARATUS

Special Paper 8

NOTE

Use Special Paper 8 for recording the decimal pyramids required by question 2.

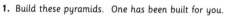

Decimal pyramids are built like this ⟶
Each number is the **total** of the two below.

1. Build these pyramids. One has been built for you.

2. Find which pyramid has the largest top number.

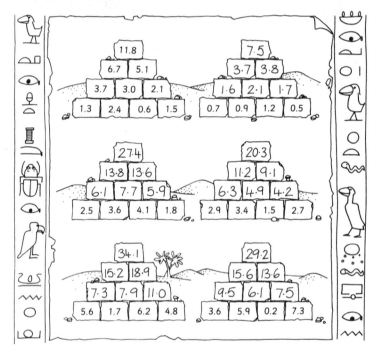

3. See how many different top numbers you can find by trying different arrangements on the bottom layer of a pyramid for the decimal numbers:
1.5, **2.4**, **3.8**, **1.6**.

3. Different arrangements of 1.5, 2.4, 3.8, 1.6, produce six different top numbers:

1.5	2.4	3.8	1.6	(21.7)
1.5	2.4	1.6	3.8	(17.3)
1.5	3.8	1.6	2.4	(20.1)
1.6	3.8	1.5	2.4	(19.9)
3.8	2.4	1.5	1.6	(17.1)
3.8	1.5	1.6	2.4	(15.5)

SPECTRUM LINKS

	Data Handling	Games	Investigations	Algebra/S&S	Number Skills
Starting					**40** Difference Pyramids
More					**11** Temperature Scales **27** Nearest 100
Go Further With	**9** Inches and Centimetres **18** Miles and Kilometres	**12** Decimate **14** Two Places **37** Four Rounds	**4** Top Brick **7** Up the Wall **20** Nearest Wholes		**4** Tenths **31** Fractions and Decimals

Decimal Pyramids

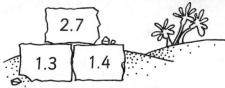

Decimal pyramids are built like this ⟶
Each number is the **total** of the two below.

1. Build these pyramids. One has been built for you.

2. Find which pyramid has the largest top number.

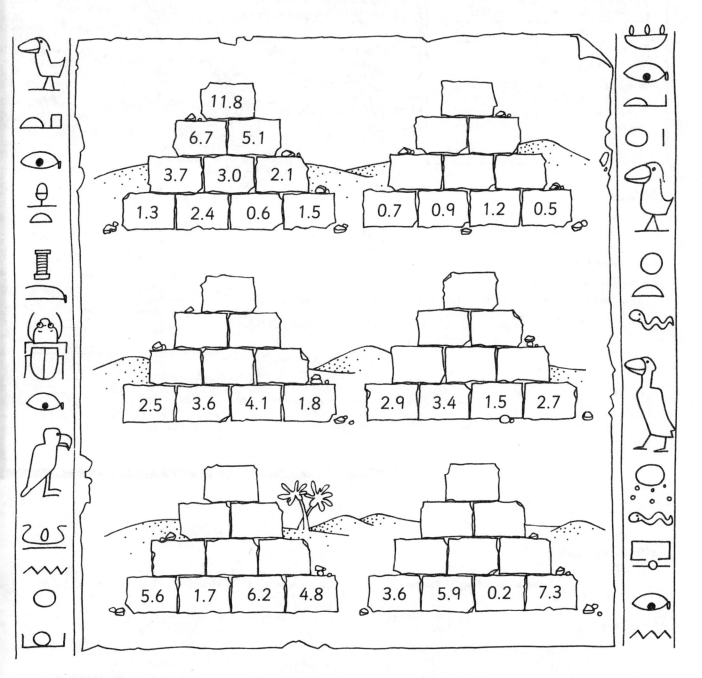

3. See how many different top numbers you can find by trying different
arrangements on the bottom layer of a pyramid for the decimal numbers:
1.5, 2.4, 3.8, 1.6.

Tower Blocks

LEVEL	UA	N	SSM	HD	A
1					
2					
3	●	●			
4	●	●			
5	●				
6					

● Addition, subtraction, multiplication and division.

SKILLS

► Finding expressions for different numbers using a restricted set of digits

EXTENSION

► Allow a choice of five digits, but insist that each expression contains at least one multiplication or division sign.

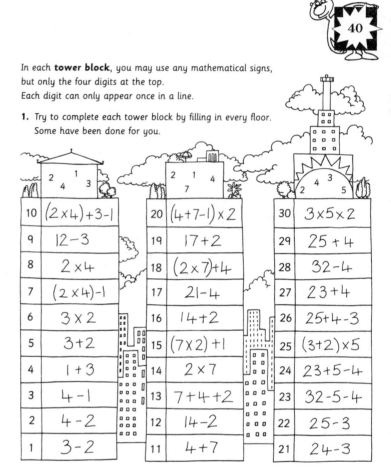

In each **tower block**, you may use any mathematical signs, but only the four digits at the top.
Each digit can only appear once in a line.

1. Try to complete each tower block by filling in every floor. Some have been done for you.

Tower 1 (digits 2 1 4 3):
10	$(2 \times 4) + 3 - 1$
9	$12 - 3$
8	2×4
7	$(2 \times 4) - 1$
6	3×2
5	$3 + 2$
4	$1 + 3$
3	$4 - 1$
2	$4 - 2$
1	$3 - 2$

Tower 2 (digits 2 1 4 7):
20	$(4 + 7 - 1) \times 2$
19	$17 + 2$
18	$(2 \times 7) + 4$
17	$21 - 4$
16	$14 + 2$
15	$(7 \times 2) + 1$
14	2×7
13	$7 + 4 + 2$
12	$14 - 2$
11	$4 + 7$

Tower 3 (digits 2 4 3 5):
30	$3 \times 5 \times 2$
29	$25 + 4$
28	$32 - 4$
27	$23 + 4$
26	$25 + 4 - 3$
25	$(3 + 2) \times 5$
24	$23 + 5 - 4$
23	$32 - 5 - 4$
22	$25 - 3$
21	$24 - 3$

2. Repeat the activity with different sets of digits for each block. Shuffle a pack of playing cards containing the numbers 1 - 9 only. Then deal out three sets of four cards to represent the digits to be used for each block.

SPECTRUM LINKS

	Data Handling	Games	Investigations	Algebra/S&S	Number Skills
Starting		**13** Big Match **18** Summary **27** Choosy	**10** Trios **12** Keep Your Balance **14** Card Tricks	**6** Shape Search **10** Stroking Cats **15** Hunt the Numbers	
More		**3** Boxer **8** Dice Superstars	**29** Asking Questions	**10** Mystery People	**15** Dice Lines **20** Equation Solving **28** Arch Numbers **31** Target Practice
Go Further With		**8** A Mouthful **33** Challenge **38** Switch	**16** Number Nine **21** Equations **33** Signs	**7** Number Tricks **10** Think of a Number **14** Whodunnit?	**6** Countdown **7** Mixed Equations **13** Three Stones

Tower Blocks

In each **tower block**, you may use any mathematical signs, but only the four digits at the top. Each digit can only appear once in a line.

1. Try to complete each tower block by filling in every floor. Some have been done for you.

Block 1 top digits: 2 1 4 3

10	
9	12 − 3
8	
7	
6	3 × 2
5	
4	
3	
2	
1	

Block 2 top digits: 2 1 4 7

20	
19	
18	
17	
16	
15	(7 × 2) + 1
14	
13	7 + 4 + 2
12	
11	

Block 3 top digits: 3 4 2 5

30	
29	
28	
27	23 + 4
26	
25	
24	
23	
22	
21	

2. Repeat the activity with different sets of digits for each block. Shuffle a pack of playing cards containing the numbers 1 - 9 only. Then deal out three sets of four cards to represent the digits to be used for each block.

Special paper 1

1	2	3	4	5	6	7	8	9	10
11	12	13	14	15	16	17	18	19	20
21	22	23	24	25	26	27	28	29	30
31	32	33	34	35	36	37	38	39	40
41	42	43	44	45	46	47	48	49	50
51	52	52	54	55	56	57	58	59	60
61	62	63	64	65	66	67	68	69	70
71	72	73	74	75	76	77	78	79	80
81	82	83	84	85	86	87	88	89	90
91	92	93	94	95	96	97	98	99	100

Special paper 2

1	2	3	4	5	6	7	8	9	10
11	12	13	14	15	16	17	18	19	20
21	22	23	24	25	26	27	28	29	30
31	32	33	34	35	36	37	38	39	40
41	42	43	44	45	46	47	48	49	50
51	52	53	54	55	56	57	58	59	60
61	62	63	64	65	66	67	68	69	70
71	72	73	74	75	76	77	78	79	80
81	82	83	84	85	86	87	88	89	90
91	92	93	94	95	96	97	98	99	100

1	2	3	4	5	6	7	8	9	10
11	12	13	14	15	16	17	18	19	20
21	22	23	24	25	26	27	28	29	30
31	32	33	34	35	36	37	38	39	40
41	42	43	44	45	46	47	48	49	50
51	52	53	54	55	56	57	58	59	60
61	62	63	64	65	66	67	68	69	70
71	72	73	74	75	76	77	78	79	80
81	82	83	84	85	86	87	88	89	90
91	92	93	94	95	96	97	98	99	100

1	2	3	4	5	6	7	8	9	10
11	12	13	14	15	16	17	18	19	20
21	22	23	24	25	26	27	28	29	30
31	32	33	34	35	36	37	38	39	40
41	42	43	44	45	46	47	48	49	50
51	52	53	54	55	56	57	58	59	60
61	62	63	64	65	66	67	68	69	70
71	72	73	74	75	76	77	78	79	80
81	82	83	84	85	86	87	88	89	90
91	92	93	94	95	96	97	98	99	100

1	2	3	4	5	6	7	8	9	10
11	12	13	14	15	16	17	18	19	20
21	22	23	24	25	26	27	28	29	30
31	32	33	34	35	36	37	38	39	40
41	42	43	44	45	46	47	48	49	50
51	52	53	54	55	56	57	58	59	60
61	62	63	64	65	66	67	68	69	70
71	72	73	74	75	76	77	78	79	80
81	82	83	84	85	86	87	88	89	90
91	92	93	94	95	96	97	98	99	100

1	2	3	4	5	6	7	8	9	10
11	12	13	14	15	16	17	18	19	20
21	22	23	24	25	26	27	28	29	30
31	32	33	34	35	36	37	38	39	40
41	42	43	44	45	46	47	48	49	50
51	52	53	54	55	56	57	58	59	60
61	62	63	64	65	66	67	68	69	70
71	72	73	74	75	76	77	78	79	80
81	82	83	84	85	86	87	88	89	90
91	92	93	94	95	96	97	98	99	100

1	2	3	4	5	6	7	8	9	10
11	12	13	14	15	16	17	18	19	20
21	22	23	24	25	26	27	28	29	30
31	32	33	34	35	36	37	38	39	40
41	42	43	44	45	46	47	48	49	50
51	52	53	54	55	56	57	58	59	60
61	62	63	64	65	66	67	68	69	70
71	72	73	74	75	76	77	78	79	80
81	82	83	84	85	86	87	88	89	90
91	92	93	94	95	96	97	98	99	100

Special paper 3

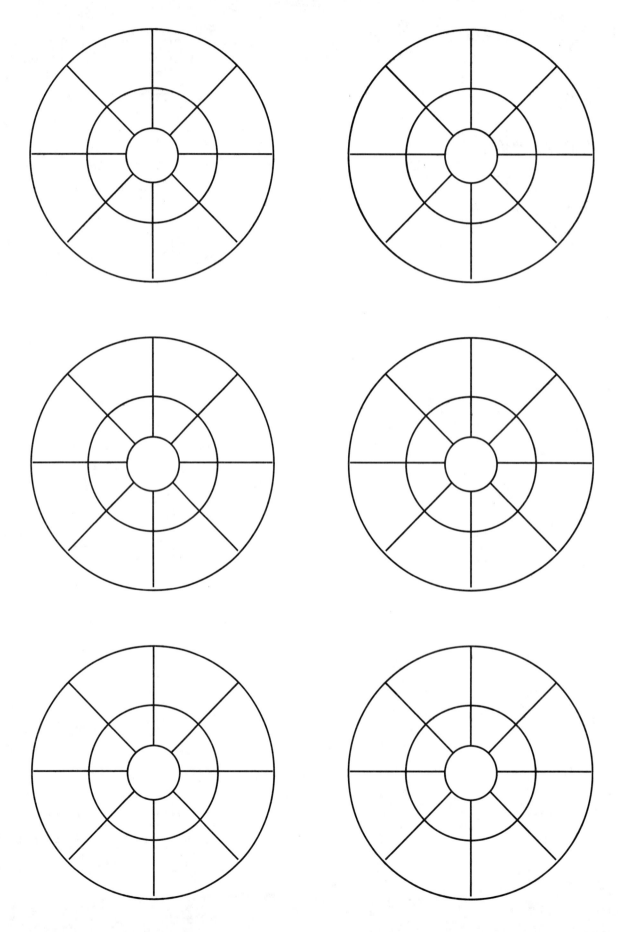

Special paper 4

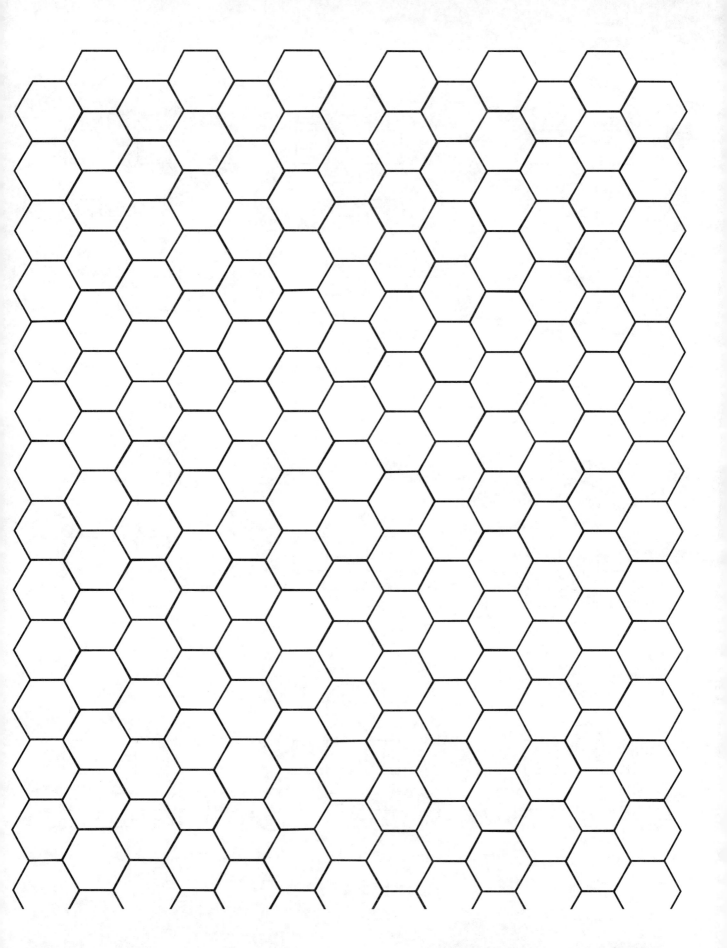

Special paper 5

Special paper 6

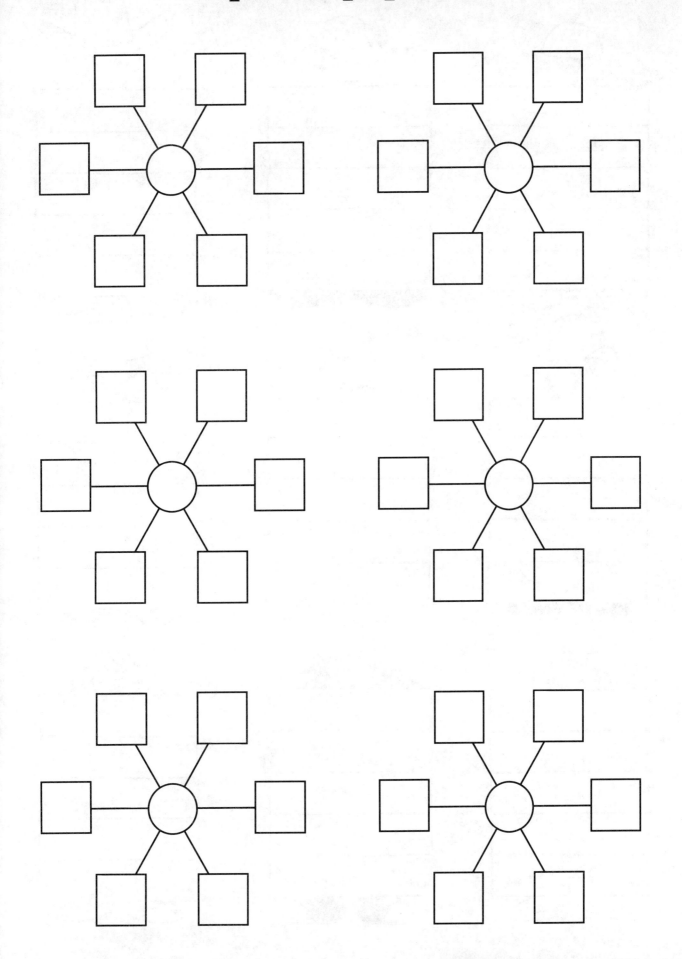

Special paper 7

SPECTRUM MATHS ■ GO FURTHER WITH NUMBER SKILLS

Special paper 8